HOME PLANS *for* OUTDOOR LIVING

HOME PLANNERS, INC.

23761 Research Drive
Farmington Hills, Michigan 48024

**PRODUCED AND DESIGNED BY
THE COMPAGE COMPANY**
San Francisco, California

Book Editor: *Philip Cecchettini*
Associate Editor: *Alice Klein*
Contributing Editor: *A. Cort Sinnes*
Developmental Editor: *Christina Nelson*
Designer: *Editorial Design / Joy Dickinson*
Photo Researchers: *Audrey Ross, Alice Klein*
Copy Editor: *Jessie Wood*

HOME PLANNERS, INC.
Charles W. Talcott, Chairman
Rickard Bailey, President & Publisher

First printing January 1988

CONTENTS

AT HOME OUTDOORS

AS TODAY'S HOMEOWNERS recognize the pleasures of coming home to the outdoors, designers of house plans are incorporating flexible outdoor living spaces directly into their designs.

Americans today value the rewards of outdoor living more than ever. The tempo of the times, the feeling of confinement that is common to many workplaces, and the dwindling amount of natural open space combine to make a multipurpose living area just outside the door one of the greatest pleasures of owning a home. It's especially satisfying to relax in the comfort and convenience of a private, personal outdoor space without having to go away for the weekend, or wait for your next vacation.

Of course, the enjoyment of indoor-outdoor living space is nothing new. Porches, courtyards, and balconies have been featured in American homes since the earliest years of this country. It's only in the past few decades, though, that patios and wood decks have come into their own as versatile indoor-outdoor spaces easily accessible from several areas of the house and adaptable to a host of activities. Sunspaces, too, have become popular in recent years. Originally intended to help reduce home fuel costs by trapping the sun's heat, they are now often incorporated into house designs as light-filled indoor rooms with an outdoor personality. Today, as homeowners all across the country recognize the delights of coming home to the outdoors, many architects and designers routinely incorporate one or more outdoor living spaces into their plans.

Predesigned house plans are a popular and successful route to home ownership. Less costly than a custom design prepared by an architect for a particular client and a particular site, predesigned or "stock" plans have been developed by architects and in most cases have already been built many times. Because they are designed with standard materials and call for standard building techniques, stock plans can easily be altered by an experienced contractor, and offer a surprising degree of flexibility for the homeowner who wishes to customize a basic plan inside or out.

Any outdoor feature adds a special dimension to the life of a house. And with a few well-chosen details—such as the fancy railing and trim that decorate this simple and functional porch—the homeowner makes a very personal statement as well.

Shopping for a house design that fulfills your personal requirements for functional, comfortable indoor-outdoor living takes considerable thought and planning, but it's well worth the effort. One way to get started is to keep a scrapbook of ideas—clippings from magazines and catalogs, ads for products that particularly appeal to you, and pictures of anything from favorite architectural styles and window shapes to planter boxes and outdoor furniture. It can be helpful, too, to talk to homeowners whose houses and gardens reflect their enjoyment of outdoor living and to take note of well-designed outdoor settings that capture your attention.

In studying the plans presented here, it's essential to evaluate not only what's needed in terms of interior arrangements—square footage, number of bedrooms, and configuration of rooms—but also to consider the adjacent outside areas and how they might be used. How does the family spend time outdoors? Does everybody like to swim, or play tennis? Will one big deck off the living area satisfy your entertaining needs, or would a series of smaller interconnected levels be more pleasing and practical? Would the indoor-outdoor atmosphere of an attached greenhouse please the gardeners in the family? Or does a busy lifestyle call for low-maintenance container gardening? What about the children's play space? Will the lawn be sufficient, or is a separate play yard a must?

New homeowners often concentrate on the interior spaces, leaving the outdoors until "later." But planning the outdoor areas at the start can save you time and money. If a concrete patio is part of the final picture, it would probably pay to have it installed when the foundation is poured. Or the hole for a side-yard spa could be dug at the same time as the house excavation.

Although the architectural styling, layout, and adjoining outdoor spaces of a particular house plan may be ideally suited to your family's likes and needs, the site itself is often the determining factor as to whether a plan can be built. In most cases it's preferable to choose the site first, and get to know its sun, shade, and wind patterns as well as its restrictions or challenges, before deciding on the final design. Sometimes, though, it's worth the effort to search for a site to accommodate a "perfect" plan, and then make compromises and adjustments as necessary.

In many cases, your contractor can handle small changes to customize your plans—substituting French doors for glass sliders, for example, or extending a plumbing line into the terrace area to accommodate a fountain or reflecting pool. Major design changes, however, usually require the services of an architect or a structural engineer.

It couldn't be simpler, yet this terrace has everything. Only a step from the house, through the shuttered French doors, it sits above the lawn and faces a ring of trees. The weathered brick floor is edged by a low wall, modest furnishings invite relaxation, and a big umbrella supplies shade. An old-fashioned greenhouse adds the final charming touch.

Many home planners and architects are sensitive to the current interest in designs that incorporate indoor-outdoor living spaces, and are careful to harmonize the outdoor areas with the exterior styling, proportions, and size of the house. The collection of plans presented in the following chapters have been chosen for such indoor-outdoor harmony. They represent a wide variety of architectural styles, from eighteenth-century Georgians and timeless Spanish ranches to wood-and-glass contemporaries of the 1980s and beyond.

To aid in making your new home a reality, a complete set of working drawings or blueprints is available for each plan shown in the book and may be ordered by referring to page 188. The plans on the following pages offer up-to-date conveniences and energy-saving features, and all are designed to maximize the pleasures of outdoor living. Some incorporate traditional elements, such as screened-in porches and entrance courtyards; others offer more recent indoor-outdoor amenities, like solar greenhouses and open-air spas.

Each chapter focuses on a different aspect of outdoor living and includes a gallery of photographs as well as a selection of plans to review. The photos do not relate directly to any one plan in this book, but they do demonstrate the ingenious ways in which other homeowners have made use of their outdoor spaces. In fact, the essays and photographs in the following chapters are intended as a resource of ideas to help you "shop" for just the right type of outdoor living space, and to underscore the advantages and pleasures of coming home to the outdoors.

PATIOS & TERRACES

CASUAL OR FORMAL, small and simple or grand in size and scale, patios and terraces are among the most popular and versatile outdoor living spaces on the American scene.

Patios and terraces are among the most flexible and convenient of all outdoor living spaces. Home plans for the 1980s and beyond reflect those qualities by integrating them into countless house designs of all sizes and styles. A patio may be a simple concrete pad, dressed up with a picnic table and some potted plants; or it may be an artful composition of intricate brickwork, carved benches, formal gardens, and a reflecting pool.

Although the terms *patio* and *terrace* are often used interchangeably, they are historically distinct. Patios and terraces evolved as separate approaches to the design of outdoor living space. Centuries ago, the patio was common in the Middle East as a kind of inner courtyard paved simply with smooth stones set into the packed earth. Around 1000 A.D. the Moors carried the idea of the patio to Spain. Spaniards who in turn migrated to the New World found a perfect use for the inner courtyard in the southern and southwestern regions of this country. Houses were then built in a rectangle or square with their outer, nearly windowless walls turned against the sun, so the bright and airy inner patio became a natural spot for outdoor living. Planted with flowers and vegetables, equipped with a well and a hearth, and made comfortable with places to sit and talk or dine, these early American patios functioned very much as they do today. But the patio did not become popular as a common feature at the back or side of virtually any kind of American house until the 1950s, when the post-war housing boom dotted the suburbs with Cape Cod cottages and single-story ranch houses.

The terrace, by contrast, evolved in the hilly terrain around the Mediterranean where it was impossible to carve a large level patiolike space from the uneven, steeply sloping ground. Terraces—from the Latin word *terra*, or earth—were originally fashioned from two or three flat plat-

You don't even have to step outside to enjoy this patio and garden: the sliding glass door reveals a lush and colorful scene and visually enlarges the interior room. A wood-paling fence supports vines, screens noise, and sturdily encloses the garden in privacy and peace.

forms of earth, each level bounded for safety by balustrades or low walls and connected by steps carved into the hillside. In ancient times, the estates of wealthy Greeks and Romans featured grand terraces with statuary and fountains, formal gardens, and carved marble balustrades and stairways. Today, grand and formal terraces are especially appropriate for houses styled in the Italian or French tradition, where wood decks might appear too casual. Like a patio, a terrace floor might be of concrete or brick or even paved with lawn—a cool, less formal alternative to masonry, but one that requires regular upkeep.

Most terraces are bounded by some type of balustrade, a feature that is not common to patios. Traditional balustrades are constructed of cast concrete or some other stone lookalike, or of brick. For a more rustic look, compatible with half-timbered Tudor style homes, balusters can be constructed of heavy wooden timbers. For contemporary exteriors, the balustrade may be of the same siding as the house.

A terrace may look more formal than a patio, and be better suited to a sloping site, but the similarities between the two outweigh the differences. The distinction is largely a matter of design and personal taste. Patios and terraces can stretch across the front or back of a house, or lie at either side. And a patio or terrace can be as formal or casual as you like. A geometric design, planned to match the scale and proportions of the house, can be quite formal. This formality can be reinforced with symmetrical planting beds and evenly spaced container plants, or by the placement of a small reflecting pool or walkway. Informal patios and terraces may have an irregular or a straight-edged contour, with casual plantings and arrangements of furniture and fixtures.

Concrete is a popular construction material for patios because it is inexpensive and relatively easy to install. Other types of masonry include brick, slate, flagstone, tile, or a combination of two or more for textural interest and aesthetic appeal. Even though the cost of concrete has increased in the past years, it still represents an excellent value compared to other building materials. Concrete is truly an all-purpose outdoor surface, capable of withstanding plenty of hard use and climatic extremes. It can be installed quickly, provides a permanent nonslip surface, and requires little upkeep.

The most common complaint about concrete patios—that they can look like parking lots—can be overcome with an exposed aggregate finish and a few colorful plants in containers or in open planting spaces. The utilitarian look of concrete can also be disguised by staining it a neutral, warm color or by embossing a pattern into the concrete while it is still wet. Using special equipment, concrete professionals can make the surface look like bricks or cobblestones.

With the addition of a few open planting areas, or several groupings of large containers, a patio or terrace is the answer for a person who doesn't go in for gardening in a big way, but doesn't want to stare out at an unrelieved expanse of concrete. These spaces can be landscaped with low-maintenance perennials, shrubs, and trees, or planted with annuals and bulbs to provide seasonal color.

The durable surface of a concrete or brick patio is also ideal for all kinds of entertaining, from an intimate dinner to a dance party to a large wedding. When you think of a patio or terrace as an additional room, the possibilities are unlimited—as long as the weather cooperates. Aside from the pleasures of outdoor living—entertaining, sunbathing, outdoor cooking—patios and terraces can also accommodate such structures as potting sheds, lath houses (good in side yards), and utility areas.

A patio can adjoin any interior room, but is particularly effective when combined with a living room, family room, or kitchen. Sliding glass or French doors help dissolve the barrier between indoors and out, effectively making the indoors seem larger, brighter, and altogether more appealing. A small patio, partially fenced or shielded with plantings, makes an ideal private refuge next to a bedroom. Private outdoor patios are an ideal way of achieving privacy and personal space in a house where the interior space is limited. Patios and terraces are among the most popular and versatile outdoor living spaces in the American home. In form they are both old and new, equally at ease with a traditional Spanish or Mediterranean design, an English country house, or a contemporary with postmodern roots.

A patio need not be adjacent to the house: this one sits across a stretch of lawn. Simple and spare, with square tiles and a low concrete wall, the patio complements the contemporary-style house. Adding a festive touch, a big umbrella provides respite from the sun.

1

2

3

4

1 *Demonstrating how flexible a patio can be, this one follows the shape of the house, first sheltered by the roof overhang, then opening out under the sky. The bricks blend well with the subdued tones of this wood-and-shingle house typical of the Pacific Northwest.*

2 *This little patio is big on desirable features: tall growth that screens the neighbors' view, attractive old brick, walls that serve as a design element and are also wide enough to sit on, flowers and a birdbath sure to bring butterflies and birds. And, of course, places to sit and enjoy it all.*

3 *Facing the interior garden court of this New Mexican house is a typical* portal, *a covered walkway that is easily accessible from many rooms. Comfortably furnished, it functions in the old Spanish way as an outdoor room.*

4 *A freeform patio surrounded by flowers makes a delightful view from above. A good example of how the harsh quality of concrete can be modified, this concrete has been etched to look like flagstones and is edged with brick. Colorful plantings and the patio's flowing shape also soften the effect.*

2

1

3

4

1, 2 *To provide comfort in the desert climate of the Southwest, a patio must offer protection from the intense sun. This house solves the problem by extending its roof system—with its vigas (main beams) and latias (smaller beams)—over the patio, but in an open way. The results: an everchanging play of light and shadow on the brick floor and a truly functional outdoor room with a magnificent view. Doors from an old hotel, furniture of weathered wood, and a settee and accessories from Mexico are details that enhance the southwestern flavor.*

3 *A patterned brick terrace departs from the traditional by using a hedge instead of a masonry balustrade. Wide and high enough to act effectively as a barrier, the hedge also provides year-round greenery, while free-standing planters add color. This large terrace is perfect for entertaining and for admiring the expansive view.*

4 *Smooth stone of different colors and shapes makes an interesting surface for this terrace, which has both formal and naturalistic elements. The gracefully contoured steps, for example, have a formal air, but are framed by rough boulders, which provide impromptu seating. The waterfall provides a focal point in this carefully designed setting.*

PLANS FEATURING PATIOS & TERRACES

The traditional charm of yesteryear is exemplified in this one-and-a-half-story home. The garage has been conveniently tucked away in the rear of the house, which makes this design ideal for a corner lot and provides privacy for the terrace at the rear of the house. The short picket fence that frames the terrace is perfectly in keeping with the overall style of the house and divides the terrace from the rest of the garden. The interior has been efficiently planned. The front living room is large and features a fireplace with a wood-box. The laundry area is accessible from both the garage and a covered side porch.

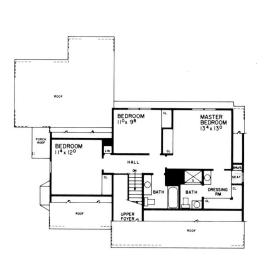

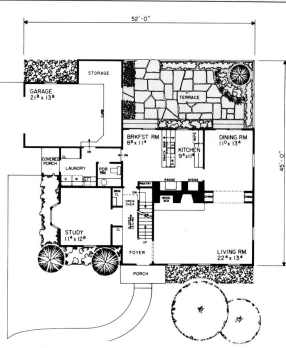

DESIGN A2658

1,218 sq. ft. — first floor
764 sq. ft. — second floor
29,690 cu. ft.

Dignified symmetry is the hallmark of this Georgian-style home. The full two-story center section is complemented by the one-and-a-half-story wings on either side. The large, formal, two-level terrace at the rear of the house is an ideal spot for gracious outdoor entertaining. The floor plan has been designed to serve an active family's needs. The gathering room, three steps down from the rest of the house, has ample space for entertaining, and opens onto the lower terrace by means of elegant French doors. This room fills an entire wing, so traffic does not pass through it. Guests and family alike will enjoy the study and formal dining rooms, which flank the foyer. Each of these rooms has a fireplace. The breakfast room, kitchen, powder room, and laundry are arranged for maximum efficiency. This area will have a light and airy atmosphere, with French doors leading to the upper terrace, and a triple window over the kitchen sink.

DESIGN A2683

2,126 sq. ft.—first floor
1,882 sq. ft.—second floor
78,828 cu. ft.

PLANS FEATURING PATIOS & TERRACES

All of the livability in this plan is in the back. Each first-floor room, except the kitchen, has access to the rear terrace via sliding glass doors to make the most of an excellent view or a pleasant garden. With a less than fifty-foot width, this plan is also ideal for a narrow lot. Two bedrooms and a lounge are on the second floor, overlooking the gathering room.

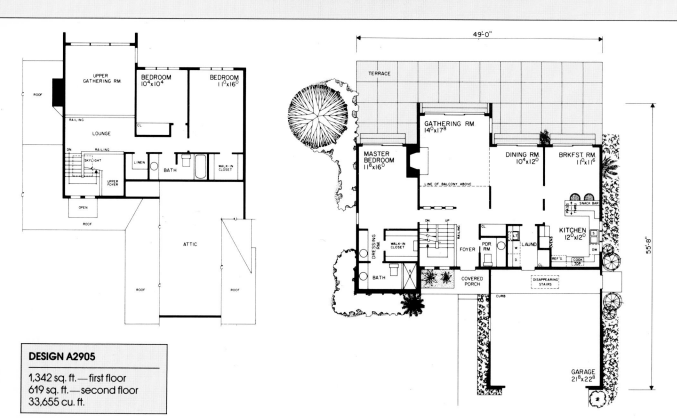

DESIGN A2905

1,342 sq. ft.—first floor
619 sq. ft.—second floor
33,655 cu. ft.

Although traditional in appearance, this modified Tudor-style home has plenty of opportunity for indoor-outdoor living. There is a large terrace accessible from both the dining and living rooms via sliding glass doors. Notice, too, the private balcony off the master bedroom. The lower level contains several practical rooms, great for entertaining or as quiet places to study. The large family room, complete with its own fireplace, bar, and powder room, has access to its own lower-level patio, with stairs connecting it to the terrace above. Plenty of diamond-paned windows and doors bring the outdoors in, even during winter months.

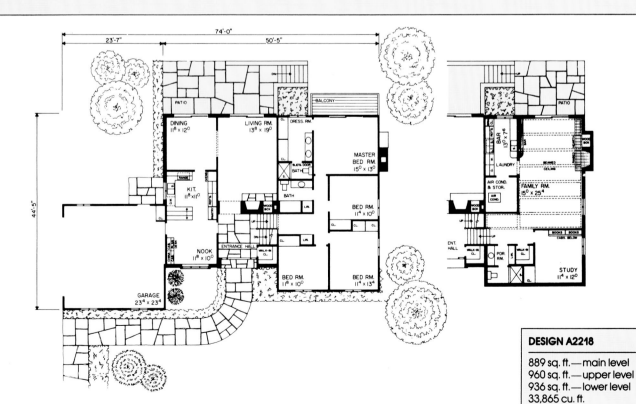

DESIGN A2218

889 sq. ft. — main level
960 sq. ft. — upper level
936 sq. ft. — lower level
33,865 cu. ft.

PATIOS & TERRACES 5

Although traditional in appearance, this modified Tudor-style home has plenty of opportunity for indoor-outdoor living. There is a large terrace accessible from both the dining and living rooms via sliding glass doors. Notice, too, the private balcony off the master bedroom. The lower level contains several practical rooms, great for entertaining or as quiet places to study. The large family room, complete with its own fireplace, bar, and powder room, has access to its own lower-level patio, with stairs connecting it to the terrace above. Plenty of diamond-paned windows and doors bring the outdoors in, even during winter months.

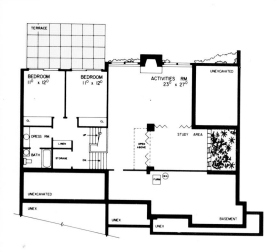

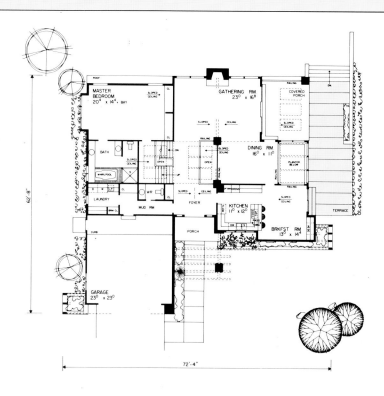

DESIGN A2936

1,980 sq. ft.—main and
　upper levels
1,475 sq. ft.—lower level
56,105 cu. ft.

PATIOS & TERRACES 6

This elegant exterior houses a very livable plan. Every bit of space has been put to good use. Note the great room, with its two-story, multi-paned window and sliding door combination offering views of a back garden. The sliding doors open onto a large, attractive terrace. The front country kitchen is efficiently planned, with a pass-through to the dining room. While the large great room will be the center of all family and entertaining activities, quiet times can be enjoyed in the front library.

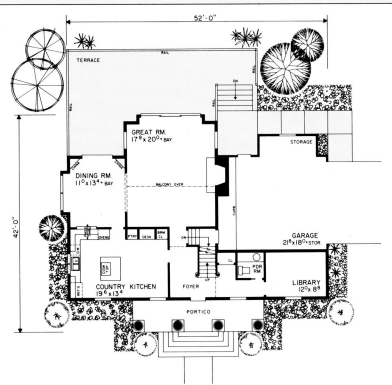

DESIGN A2668

1,206 sq. ft.—first floor
1,254 sq. ft.—second floor
47,915 cu. ft.

PATIOS & TERRACES 7

This striking contemporary house is basically one-room wide. From the front, it presents an impressive facade, complete with a modern covered porch. Owing to its unique design, all of the major rooms face the rear of the house and provide access to a huge terrace and balcony. This house would make the most of a lot with a view of a forest, the seaside, or a sweeping prairie.

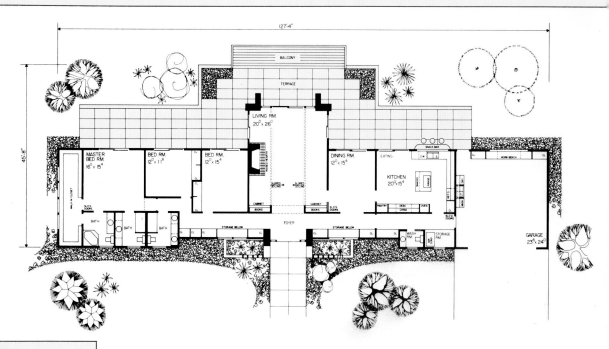

DESIGN A2256

2,632 sq. ft.
35,023 cu. ft.

PATIOS & TERRACES 8

This traditional ranch-style house has been designed to make the most of a hillside or sloping lot. One story in the front becomes two in the rear, allowing for a ground-level patio as well as a large deck off the living room, dining room, and breakfast area. In addition, the deck serves as an overhead for the patio, offering cooling shade to the rooms below. Note the expanse of multi-paned windows across the rear of the house, inviting use of both the patio and deck.

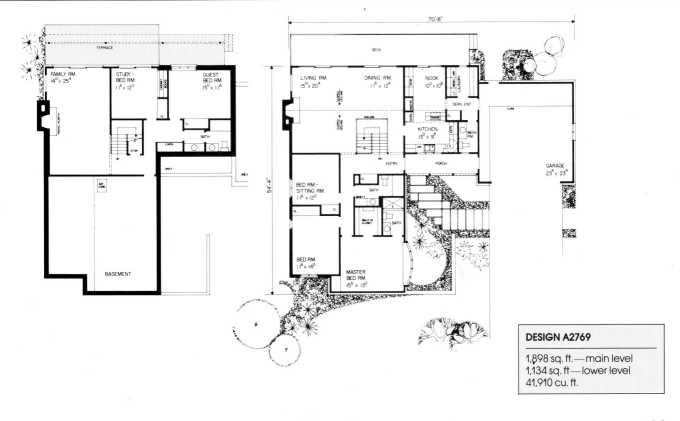

DESIGN A2769

1,898 sq. ft.—main level
1,134 sq. ft—lower level
41,910 cu. ft.

PATIOS & TERRACES 9

This traditional two-story home is a fine example of mid-18th-century design. It features a warm brick facade, a steeply pitched roof broken by two chimneys at each end, pedimented dormers, and front and rear covered porches. The rear porch leads to a large terrace, which is easily accessible from the family room, kitchen, and main entrance hall. Inside, Georgian details lend elegance, including turned balusters and a curved banister ornament on the formal staircase.

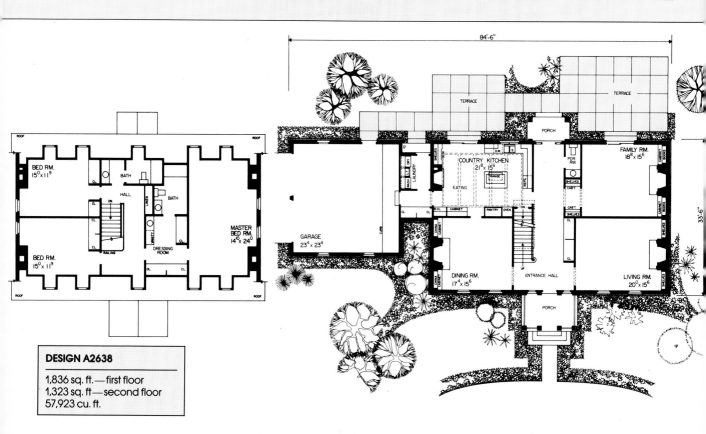

DESIGN A2638

1,836 sq. ft.—first floor
1,323 sq. ft.—second floor
57,923 cu. ft.

This striking contemporary design offers plenty of opportunities for leisure living both outdoors and in. Terraces on two different levels, two separate balconies, and plenty of floor-to-ceiling windows and skylights allow for indoor-outdoor living in any season. The house is built on three levels and includes an activities room with a bar, an exercise room with a sauna, and two gathering rooms.

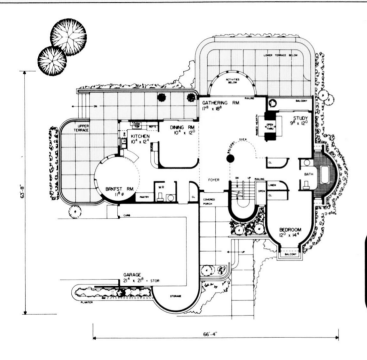

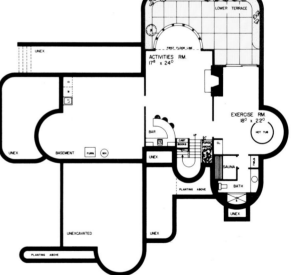

DESIGN A2926

1,570 sq. ft. — first floor
598 sq. ft. — second floor
1,080 sq. ft. — lower level
42,114 cu. ft.

PLANS FEATURING PATIOS & TERRACES

This contemporary home with traditional details has an unusual cross-shaped plan, providing both privacy and shelter for its outdoor living spaces. Patios on both sides of the house provide different exposures for different times of the day. Note how the family room provides access to both patios—perfect for entertaining. The cross-shaped design makes for easy family living and pays special attention to traffic patterns.

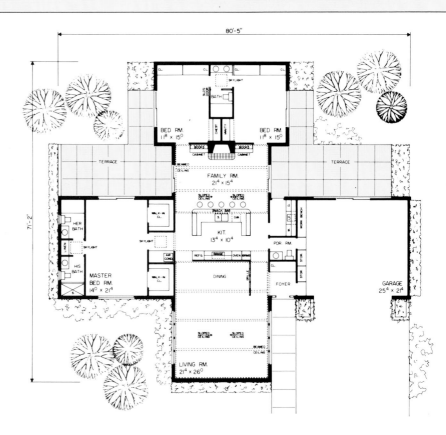

DESIGN A2244

2,489 sq. ft.
30,196 cu. ft.

PATIOS & TERRACES 12

Two one-story wings flank the two-story center section of this design, which is reminiscent of 18th-century tidewater Virginia homes. The unique L-shape provides privacy for the rear terrace, a handsome and appropriate addition to this traditional design. Access to the terrace is provided by multi-paned sliding glass doors off the family room and living room. Inside, the left wing is a huge living room; the right wing has a master bedroom suite, service area, and garage. The kitchen, dining room, and family room are centrally located, with three bedrooms above.

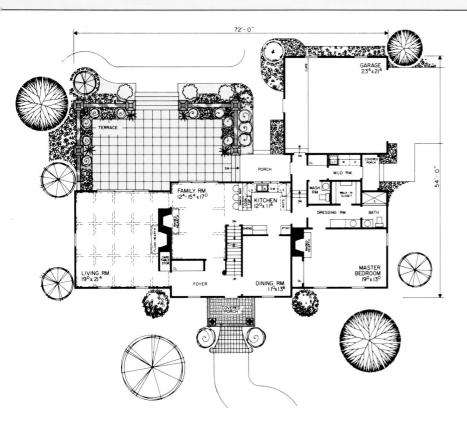

DESIGN A2667

1,827 sq. ft.—first floor
697 sq. ft.—second floor
46,290 cu. ft.

DECKS

A WELL-DESIGNED DECK can blend with virtually any style house and expand the livability of adjoining rooms. It can also transform a hilly or problem site into an inviting outdoor environment.

Wood decks have gained popularity in recent years, and for good reason. For a relatively modest investment of time and money, decks dramatically increase the livability of a house. They bridge the gap between indoors and out, providing a transition zone that is part house, part garden. Decks are highly versatile living spaces that can go anywhere around the house—in front, at the back or side, off a second story, or even on the roof. They can be constructed on one or more levels and in practically any shape, and can expand the potential of virtually any room in the house.

One of the advantages of decks is that they can usually be built at the same level as the adjacent interior floor. At first glance this feature may not seem important, but sliding glass doors or French doors opening directly onto the outdoor space—without steps up or down—effectively make a deck an extension of the room.

Decks can be the ideal solution to uneven terrain, an irregular lot, or a problem site. A yard that slopes away from the house, or one that's divided by a gully or an outcropping of rocks, may be difficult to use effectively and seem impossible to landscape. A multilevel deck system, connected by stairs, ramps, or bridges, can turn an underused yard into a comfortable, spacious, and inviting outdoor environment. If the area available is odd-shaped, the deck can be designed to fit the space—a real advantage where mature trees and rock formations are part of the existing landscape. A well-designed deck can be integrated with nearly any style house in almost any location. Railings may be fashioned to match the house trim, as on a traditional Georgian or New England farmhouse design; or the deck itself can be contoured to echo the angles of a window bay or the curve of the turret on a Tudor or Victorian house. In fact, a deck doesn't have to have a conventional open railing at all. The railing

The addition of this ebony railing, striking in its simplicity and its subtle shape, turns a deck into a work of art.

may be enclosed to form a solid partial wall—wood on the inside to match the floor, perhaps, but stuccoed, shingled, or painted on the outside to work with the house exterior.

A deck can function in the same way as any room it adjoins. As a rule of thumb, such a deck should be about the same size and shape as the adjoining room. A deck off a kitchen can become an outdoor cooking area; next to a dining room, it's easily accessible for al fresco dining. Decks off living rooms and bedrooms make the adjoining rooms seem larger by offering outdoor living space with all the comforts of home close at hand. One of the most popular deck locations is adjacent to the kitchen/dining area. Outfitted with a table and chairs, a grill, and perhaps even a sink, the deck can function like a second kitchen and dining room during the warm months of the year. Furthermore, a deck off the kitchen makes a great play space for the kids, where Mom or Dad can keep an eye on them while working indoors. With the addition of a portable gate, even toddlers and pets can be easily monitored.

A single deck with access to several rooms makes a versatile multi-functional living area. If the deck is spacious, or built in levels, furnishings, planters, and lighting may be arranged to create separate areas—

French doors open onto a sunny terrace, which leads to a deck shaded by a vine-covered pergola. The deck solves the problem of how to gain more outdoor living space on irregular land.

comfortable seating grouped near the living room, for example, and table and chairs placed close to the kitchen or dining room. Thoughtful placement of furnishings can make the space at once more functional and livable and improve circulation from room to room.

If you are lucky enough to have a building site with an exceptional view, or one that is wooded with mature trees, consider a deck as a way of maximizing the potential of your home. When elevated above the ground, a deck can afford a vantage point from which to appreciate a view. On a wooded lot, it can put you amid the tree branches and their protective beauty. And decks are comparatively easy to construct *around* trees without harming them. Some decks are not attached to the house in the conventional way. A bridge, walkway, or steps of wood or masonry might lead to a detached deck that takes advantage of another view or nestles in a grove of trees, harmonizing with the natural setting. Equipped simply with benches built around a tree trunk or dressed up with a gazebo, this kind of deck can maximize the pleasures of outdoor living.

A windscreen of wood or glass, or even a wooden lattice fence planted with vines, will offer considerable protection in a windy location. A deck with a south or west exposure, protected from the wind on one or more sides by the house yet open to the sun's warmth, can be a real boon for both plants and people, especially during winter. However, a deck with a sunny disposition needs a deep roof overhang, an overhead trellis, or a well-placed deciduous tree to temper the summer sun with shade.

Most decks are ideal for plants in containers. You may be satisfied with a couple of containers for seasonal color; or you may want a complete container garden of flowers and vegetables. Just be sure that the deck can support the weight of the soil-filled, water-drenched containers. Elevate containers an inch or so off the deck floor to prevent water stains and rot damage.

Decks lend themselves beautifully to the addition of a hot tub or spa. Acrylic or fiberglass spas normally require some excavation and sit directly in the hole at ground level. So installed, they are suited to decks constructed on or near the ground. Wood hot tubs, on the other hand, should not come in direct contact with the earth, and so make an excellent choice for elevated decks. Hot tubs require an engineered foundation to provide adequate support and drainage, regardless of whether they project above the deck surface or lie flush with the floor.

The plans in this chapter show decks of all shapes and sizes in conjunction with a wide variety of house styles and in many different situations. Whatever style you choose, your deck is sure to be one of the most lived-in rooms outside your house.

DECKS

1 *One of the best things about a deck is how it can convert uneven, hard-to-use terrain into useful space. This simple, two-level deck is multipurpose: steps lead up to a spa and down to the ground, and there's plenty of room for all sorts of activity, including sunbathing, eating, and relaxing.*

2 *The possibilities for decks are endless: a picket fence gives this deck an old-fashioned, countrified feeling.*

3

2

1

4

5

3   *After hugging the side of this Connecticut shingle house, the deck suddenly opens out next to the bay, becoming large enough to accommodate some outdoor furniture. You can sit anywhere along the deck, however, on the bench that runs the entire length of the railing. The railing itself is both sturdy and open, and hints at the design of the widow's walk atop the roof.*

4   *From your comfortable chaise on the deck, you can enjoy a picturesque progression from stone-edged spa, to gracefully shaped pool, to lawn and garden beyond. The wood deck dries quickly and provides a non-slip surface for bathers; aggregate surrounds the larger pool.*

5   *A steep slope is no longer a problem with a deck; in fact, if you're lucky enough to have a wooded lot, a deck can literally put you among the treetops. With its built-in bench, this shady corner is a good place for time out.*

1 *Decks can be designed to harmonize with any house style—even traditional. Here is a unique deck, integrated in all its details—from the soft gray weathered boards to the detailed railings—with a very traditional house. With the pergola-like roof extension (covered with plexiglass), the deck works like a porch—and, with the shades and curtains pulled, like an enclosed room. A fully equipped kitchen with a built-in barbecue makes this outdoor room an ideal place to dine.*

1

2

3

4

2   *Decks are adaptable. This one takes on an unusual shape as it wraps around the trees, perching among them like a treehouse. Weathered wood boards and simple wooden chairs are natural to this rustic setting.*

3   *Here's a great example of how a deck at the same level as an interior room can extend that room's space, visually and practically. Seen through large picture windows and a sliding glass door, this deck was built to take in a wonderful panorama and offer a superior vantage point for sunsets.*

4   *Unusually long and narrow, this terrace-like deck separates cultivated lawn from the yard's more wild growth, and gives an otherwise quiet area a bright focal point with its containers of assorted azaleas. An extension spans sloping ground and reclaims more space for human activity.*

PLANS FEATURING DECKS

DECKS 1

This plan would be good for a building site close to water—either on a lake or at a marina—or backing up to a golf course. It is designed to maximize outdoor living in the rear of the house, by means of a huge deck off the living-dining area and kitchen—complete with a pass-through window to use as an outdoor snack bar. The deck offers plenty of room for sunbathing, dining, or entertaining, with easy access to the large living room via a bank of sliding glass doors.

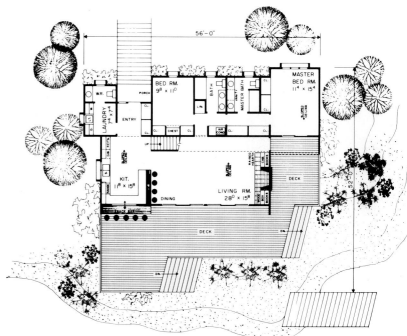

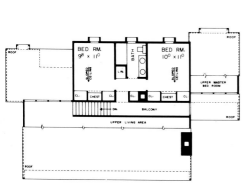

DESIGN A2472

1,384 sq. ft.—first floor
436 sq. ft.—second floor
22,127 cu. ft.

DECKS 2

The streetside facade of this contemporary design belies the amount of outdoor living space provided at the rear of the house. With its large, unusually shaped deck off the gathering room, dining room, and breakfast room; its ground-level patio; and its private balcony off the master suite—this is a house with plenty of space and privacy both indoors and out.

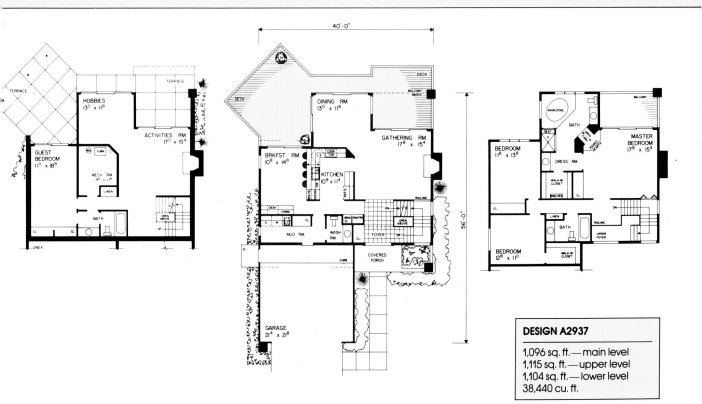

DESIGN A2937

1,096 sq. ft.—main level
1,115 sq. ft.—upper level
1,104 sq. ft.—lower level
38,440 cu. ft.

DECKS 3

A contemporary house with an accent on outdoor living. Three balconies, a huge deck, and a large patio provide diverse locations for all types of outdoor activities. The style and design of this house are good for a hillside or sloping lot—especially one with an attractive view to the rear. This plan would also work well with a swimming pool. Note how the upper deck partially shades the patio—perfect for sunbathing above and for cooling off below.

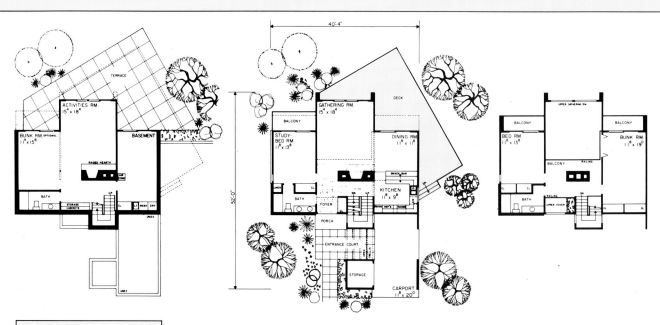

DESIGN A2511

1,043 sq. ft.—main level
703 sq. ft.—upper level
794 sq. ft.—lower level
30,528 cu. ft.

Mediterranean-style homes have always opened themselves to the outdoors, and this design is no exception. It features a good division of space that is ideal for active families: informal living takes place on the lower level in the family room, lounge, and adjoining patio. A more formal setting is found on the upper level, with living and dining rooms sharing a through-fireplace, and a good-sized deck that is ideal for warm-weather entertaining.

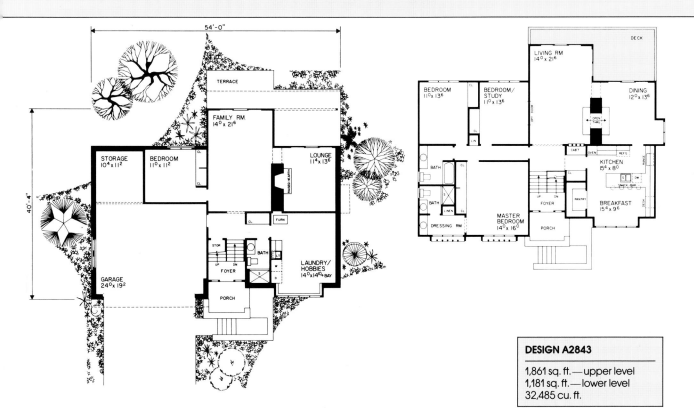

DESIGN A2843

1,861 sq. ft.—upper level
1,181 sq. ft.—lower level
32,485 cu. ft.

DECKS 5

The street view of this contemporary design features a small courtyard entrance and a private terrace off the study—two outstanding areas for intimate outdoor living. This design features spacious first-floor activity areas that flow smoothly into each other. In the gathering room a raised-hearth fireplace creates a dramatic focal point. An adjacent covered terrace, featuring a skylight, is ideal for outdoor dining and could be screened in later as an additional room.

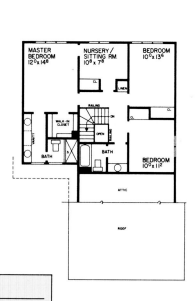

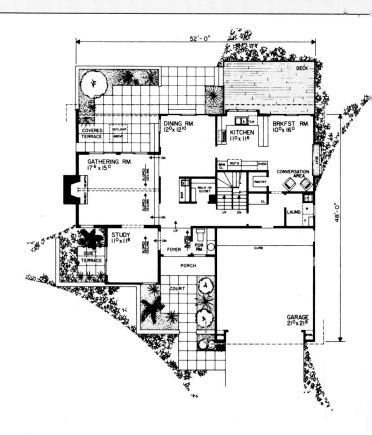

DESIGN A2823

1,370 sq. ft.—first floor
927 sq. ft.—second floor
34,860 cu. ft.

DECKS 6

An unusual bi-level design sets this traditional Tudor house apart from other plans. Good for family living, it features a split foyer, which provides access to both levels. The breakfast room, kitchen, and dining room, all on the upper level, have access to the second-story deck. Directly below, the family room opens onto a large patio. The overhead deck provides shade for a portion of the patio. Note the covered front porch—an ideal spot for relaxing. Three bedrooms are on the upper level, a fourth on the lower.

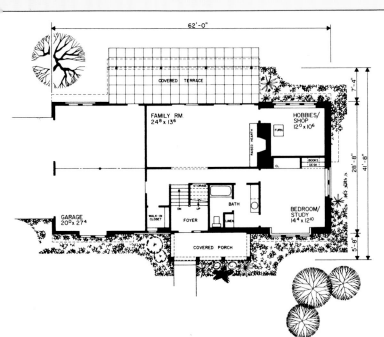

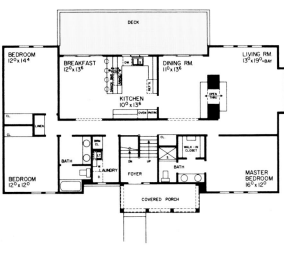

DESIGN A2844

1,882 sq. ft.—upper level
1,168 sq. ft.—lower level
37,860 cu. ft.

PLANS FEATURING DECKS

DECKS 7

This one-story contemporary ranch-style home doubles its livability by means of a large deck and a terrace that is partially covered by the deck. The living room, dining room, and breafast nook have access to the deck, making it perfect for outdoor eating and entertaining. The terrace is accessible from a study and activities room, ideal for the younger set.

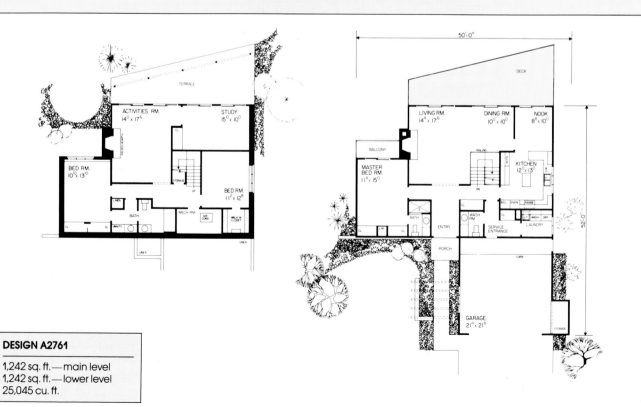

DESIGN A2761

1,242 sq. ft.—main level
1,242 sq. ft.—lower level
25,045 cu. ft.

DECKS 8

Although not a huge house, this design is long on livability—a house to enjoy life in. With its wide overhanging hip roof, the unadorned facade has an appealing simplicity. The spacious living-dining area is one of the focal points of the plan. The large areas of glass and the accessibility, through sliding glass doors, of the outdoor balcony are important features. For recreation, there is a lower-level area that opens onto a large terrace, which is partially shaded by the balcony above.

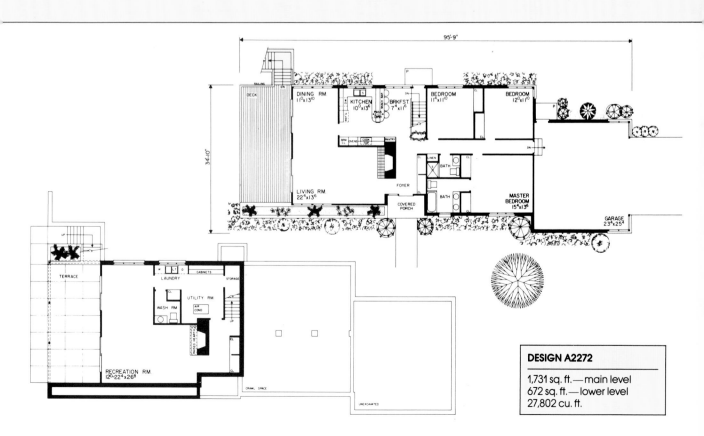

DESIGN A2272

1,731 sq. ft.—main level
672 sq. ft.—lower level
27,802 cu. ft.

DECKS 9

Outdoors-oriented families will appreciate the multiple sliding glass doors and sweeping decks that make this contemporary house so livable. The plan of the first floor features a spacious two-story gathering room with a sloping ceiling, a large fireplace, and access to the large deck that runs the full length of the house. Also directly off the deck is the dining room, which is half-open to the second floor above. The second floor is brightened by a skylight and houses two bedrooms with access to a balcony, plus a lounge and a full bath.

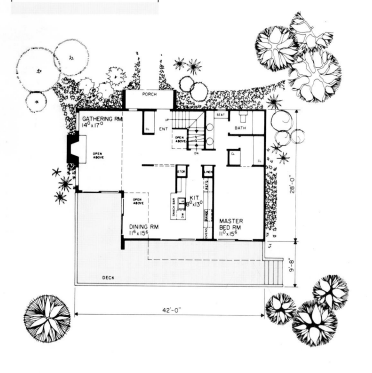

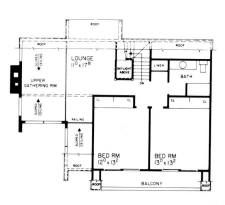

DESIGN A2489

1,076 sq. ft.—first floor
693 sq. ft.—second floor
33,185 cu. ft.

44

DECKS 10

A cozy cottage, ideal for use as a full-time home or as a lakeside or mountain retreat. The gathering room features floor-to-peaked-ceiling windows, perfect for framing an attractive view. The deck, off the nearby dining room, is an ideal spot to take outdoor meals during warm weather. The upper floor has two sizable bedrooms, a full bath, and a lounge area overlooking the gathering room below. The first-floor master suite is good-sized and well appointed.

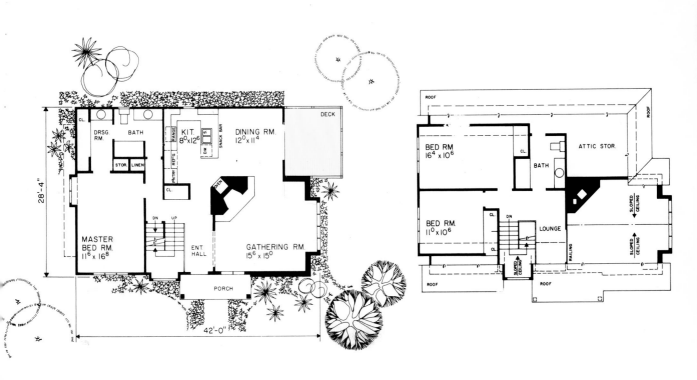

DESIGN A2488

1,113 sq. ft.—first floor
543 sq. ft.—second floor
36,055 cu. ft.

PORCHES

FOR SUMMERTIME SITTING, lemonade sipping, or rainy day games, porches have long been a favorite for outdoor living under cover of a roof. Even a small porch can greatly increase a home's livability.

Americans love a porch: stretching across the back of the house, wrapping around the front, projecting to the side; screened-in, glassed-in, or wide open to the outdoors. Before air-conditioning, the front porch was the place to find shade and a little breeze, a comfortable place to sit and a vantage point to view the passing scene. After the supper dishes were dried and put away, the porch was the place to sit and talk softly into the night. The front porch facilitated neighborly conversations in the most informal and spontaneous way. In many parts of the country, summertime porch-sitting is still a way of life.

It's little wonder, then, that for many people a house just isn't a home unless it has a porch. In its simplest form a porch is little more than a stoop—a small covered area that offers protection at the back or front door. At its grandest, a porch may wrap all the way around the house, form an L-shape, or span the entire front or back of the house. Large porches make even modest-sized houses seem much larger, increase architectural significance, and add valuable outdoor space for sitting, reading, eating, visiting, or snoozing, usually at a fraction of the cost of an interior room of the same size.

A porch can be incorporated into virtually any house plan, although it is most often associated with traditional styles—southern cottage, midwestern farmhouse, or the typical ranch house of the Old West. Contemporary-style homes can have porches, too, without sacrificing the integrity of the design. In fact, until recent years, when smaller lots and busier streets forced homeowners to move outdoor living to the rear patio, the porch was a common feature on houses of all types and sizes. Classical architecture made use of porches as well as courtyards and atriums for indoor-outdoor living. In other parts of the world, porches evolved as outdoor living and sleeping areas under a shady overhanging

A small porch not only offers shelter but can sometimes make a grand entrance as well.

roof system. The bungalows of India used wraparound verandas to keep inhabitants cool both day and night, and in the Orient, the porch could be converted to interior space with the help of movable screens.

In our country, from the 1700s on, southern houses built in the French tradition enjoyed long and ample second-story balconylike porches called *galleries*. Located well above the damp ground and insect population, open to the breezes, and accessible from every room, these porches served multiple purposes as women sewed, children played, and everyone conversed, relaxed, and cooled off. By the mid-1800s, porches were popular all over America, appearing on farmhouses, shingled Victorians, and Greek Revival styles. Even the most modest urban designs took advantage of the practical stoop or a small porch at one side. In the 1950s the spacious front porch vanished to make room for larger interior spaces, and the back porch gave way to the patio. Happily though, with the renewed interest in historic architecture and traditional house styles, the American porch is making a comeback.

The return in popularity of the porch has also led to the return of many types of porch furnishings, from the old-fashioned porch swing to wood, wicker, and metal recreations of period chairs and tables. The homeowner of the 1980s can combine furnishings and accessories—a rocking chair, planter boxes brimming with colorful flowers, an antique umbrella stand—to reflect personal tastes and echo the style of the house, creating a first impression that sets the tone for the home's interior. In fact, a large front porch graced with comfortable furnishings and plants invites visitors to linger.

A porch is a welcome haven of retreat from a storm, a spot to discard boots and raincoats and let umbrellas drip dry. It's the perfect place to store firewood, dry and close at hand. And more than one rained-out birthday party has been rescued by a handy porch. Because their wall and floor surfaces are more durable than those indoors, porches are ideal for child-oriented projects and crafts. It may not be possible to hose down an inside room after a poster-painting spree, but on a porch it makes perfect sense.

Back porches tend to be more private than those at the front of the house. A back porch can be a cool, shady place to grow shade-loving plants, a reprieve from a sun-soaked patio, or the perfect spot to put a barbecue grill for year-round use. Back porches that connect with kitch-

With the added protection of an extended side wall, this porch in Santa Fe, New Mexico, makes a fine outdoor living room: shady, cool, and out of the wind.

ens or family rooms are ideal for warm-weather outdoor eating. A small covered utility porch at the side of the house, off a kitchen or laundry, is a handy place to drop off groceries, feed pets, store garden tools, and take off muddy boots.

Screened-in porches are favorites in areas plagued by insects during the warm months. A screened porch provides the best of both worlds: the fresh air, sights, and sounds of the outdoors along with the protection of an interior room. A screened porch is a wonderful place to eat, read, or just lounge about, and is often the preferred spot for sleeping during hot spells. Furnished with a small dining table, a few comfortable chairs, and a daybed with plenty of pillows, a screened-in porch may become the most-used room in the house during the warm season.

This glassed-in porch, with its charming, old-fashioned furniture, is a totally protected, all-season living space.

The addition of glass to a porch changes its character completely. While it still offers the sight of the great outdoors, the glassed-in porch is a protected spot, more like a garden room or a sunspace. With proper glazing and ventilation, the porch can be used all year. Some homeowners opt for a screened porch with removable glass panels to offer seasonal protection.

Like porches, breezeways are roof-covered extensions of the indoor environment. However, their primary function is to serve as connectors or passageways. Most often a breezeway links a house to a garage, but it may also connect a house to a guest wing, a recreation room, or even a bar. Practically speaking, these covered walkways offer protection from the elements as one passes from one area to another. In a cold climate, they may even be enclosed in safety glass.

In terms of outdoor living, a breezeway makes a good place for hanging baskets, particularly for shade-loving plants such as fuchsias, tuberous begonias, and impatiens. If the corridor is made a little wider than normal, the walkway becomes a good play area for children, especially during rainy weather. A bench or two can serve as a dropping-off spot for bags of groceries or other loads of household goods.

Perhaps the best thing about porches is that they offer a place to get away from it all without going very far. Whether you want to cool off after mowing the lawn or warm up in the morning sun, a porch is an important part of what makes a house a home.

1

2

1   With a spacious front porch that wraps around to one side, and a smaller porch on the other side, this Victorian house has a porch for every purpose. You can pass the time of day with neighbors from the front porch swing, or you can retreat to a side area for more privacy.

2   For climates where rain and insects are plenty, a screened-in porch may be the answer.

3

3 *Here's an unlikely—but successful—combination: a rustic summer cottage in the imposing Greek Revival style. The wraparound porch is nearly as big as the house itself.*

4 *This modern California farmhouse boasts a porch that wraps around all four sides, so there is always a place to get out of—or into—the sunshine. The porch style could not be more perfectly integrated with the overall clean-lined design of the house.*

4

PORCHES

1 *Not only does this full front porch provide ample room for rocking and chatting; its many staunch columns hold up a substantial roof system and make a grand and dignified entrance way.*

2 *A cousin to the porch, the breezeway is a covered passageway, usually linking the house and garage. In this contemporary Connecticut house, based on the traditional New England farmhouse, the breezeway, with its little pitched roof, echoes the architecture of both buildings.*

3 *The spirit of the Southwest seems to emanate from the simple and functional porch of this adobe house.*

1

2

3

PORCHES 1

This home reflects the Greek Revival heritage so popular in this country generations ago. The front and rear porticos have graceful columns, and are sure to beckon family and friends to wander outside and "sit a spell." While the exterior comes from yester-year, the floor plan is designed to serve today's active family. A wide variety of activities can be enjoyed in the huge gathering room that stretches from the front to the rear of the house. Three bedrooms are on the second floor.

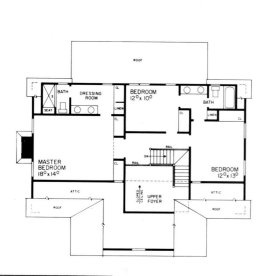

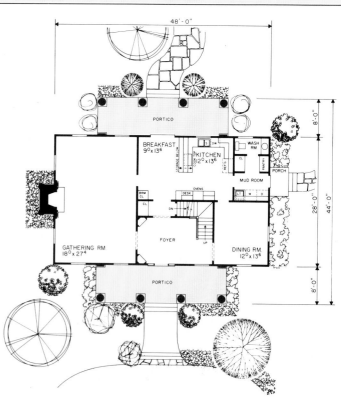

DESIGN A2663

1,344 sq. ft.—first floor
947 sq. ft.—second floor
39,790 cu. ft.

PORCHES 2

This Georgian-style house presents a pleasing facade to the street, with its full-front covered porch supported by twelve-inch-diameter wooden columns. A porch of this size is sure to be well used. The garage wing has a sheltered service entry and brick facing that complements the overall design. Sliding glass doors link the terrace and family room, providing an indoor-outdoor area for entertaining (see the rear elevation). The floor plan has been designed to serve the family efficiently. The stairway in the foyer leads to four second-floor bedrooms. The third floor is windowed and can be used as a study and studio area.

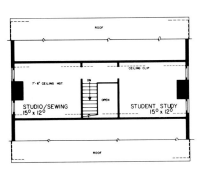

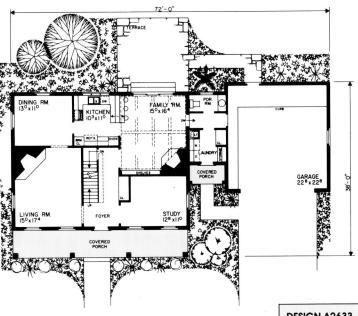

DESIGN A2633

1,338 sq. ft. — first floor
1,200 sq. ft. — second floor
506 sq. ft. — third floor
44,525 cu. ft.

PLANS FEATURING PORCHES

PORCHES 3

Historically referred to as a "half house," this authentic adaptation has its roots in New England architecture. With the completion of the second floor, the house would double its sleeping capacity. Both the family and living rooms have a fireplace, and the plan features a covered breezeway, significantly enhancing the facade of the house while offering shelter between the garage and the house. Many built-in units are featured throughout the plan.

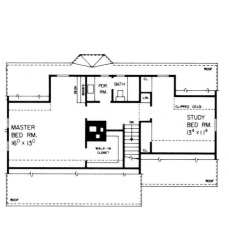

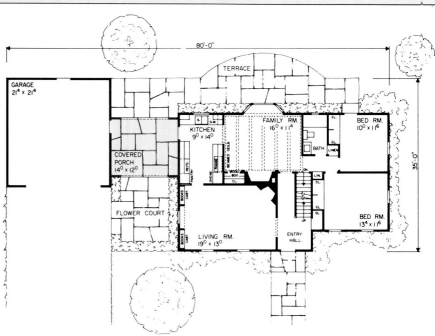

DESIGN A2146

1,182 sq. ft.—first floor
708 sq. ft.—second floor
28,303 cu. ft.

PORCHES 4

This appealing farmhouse is complemented by an inviting front porch running the entire length of the house— and a matching one to the rear. A nice-sized study is to the right of the entrance, and a spacious living room to the left. The adjacent dining room has an attractive bay window and is a step away from the efficient kitchen. The large family room has a snack bar for entertaining. A powder room and laundry are also on the first floor. Upstairs, a master bedroom suite features a bath with an oversized tub and shower and a dressing room. Also on this floor are two bedrooms, a full bath, and a large attic.

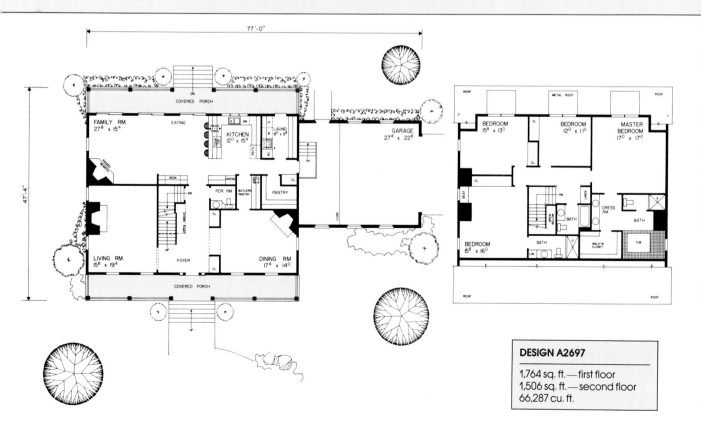

DESIGN A2697

1,764 sq. ft.—first floor
1,506 sq. ft.—second floor
66,287 cu. ft.

PLANS FEATURING PORCHES

PORCHES 5

This two-story design is based on the 18th-century homestead of Secretary of Foreign Affairs John Jay. It is filled with the special touches of a fine family home. The two large covered porches, front and rear, recall an era when the pace was slower and there was time to enjoy the pleasures of porch-sitting. Note the three fireplaces—in the living room, library, and country kitchen—the large master bath, and the "clutter room" adjoining the equally practical mudroom.

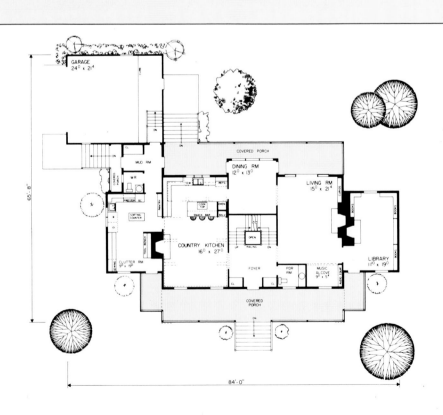

DESIGN A2694

2,026 sq. ft.—first floor
1,386 sq. ft.—second floor
69,445 cu. ft.

This design has its roots in the South, where it is referred to as a "raised cottage." This adaptation has front and rear covered porches for informal enjoyment. The columns that support the porch roofs are in a modified Greek Revival style. Note how the set-back garage provides protection and privacy for the back porch. Flanking the center foyer are the formal living room and library and the informal country kitchen. The fireplace in the library and the whirlpool bath in the master-suite bathroom are other special features.

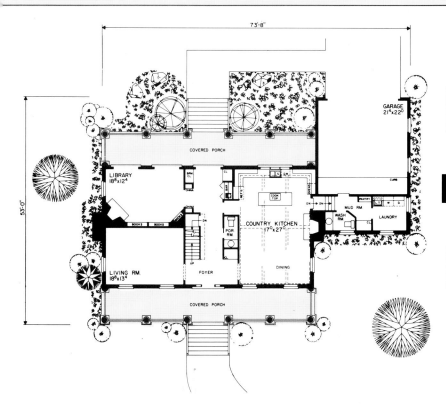

DESIGN A2686

1,683 sq. ft.—first floor
1,541 sq. ft.—second floor
57,345 cu. ft.

PORCHES 7

This traditional one-story design offers all the economical benefits of shared living space without sacrificing privacy, along with a large covered rear porch complete with skylights. The 680-square-foot common area is made up of the great room, dining room, and kitchen. The sloping ceiling in this area creates an open feeling, as do the sliding glass doors on each side of the fireplace, leading to the back porch. Separate outdoor entrances lead to each of the sleeping wings. Additional space is found in the basement, which is the full size of the common area. The covered porch and the garage with additional storage space are other features.

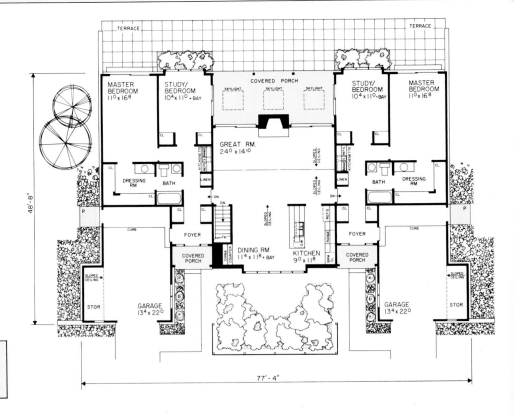

DESIGN A2869

1,986 sq. ft.
48,455 cu. ft.

PORCHES 8

The exterior of this full two-story is highlighted by the covered front porch and the covered second-floor balcony, both of which run the full length of the house. The terrace at the rear of the house adjoins the dining room and kitchen, making it an easy place to serve outdoor meals. Sleeping facilities are on the second floor. All four bedrooms are good-sized, and the spacious master bath deserves special note.

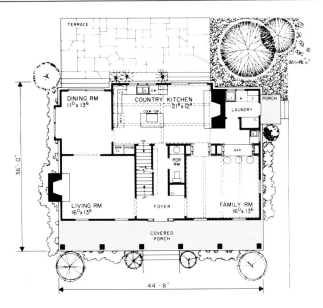

DESIGN A2664

1,308 sq. ft.—first floor
1,262 sq. ft.—second floor
49,215 cu. ft.

PORCHES 9

This high-styled design is truly distinctive. The appealing roof line, the window treatment, the arched openings, and the stucco exterior set the character of this two-story home. The covered front porch is ideal for outdoor living and provides sheltered entry to the spacious foyer. From this point, traffic patterns flow efficiently to all areas. The family room–laundry zone is one step below the main level. The kitchen is flanked by two eating areas; both overlook the rear garden. Each of the two large living areas features a fireplace, sliding glass doors, and a covered porch. Upstairs there are four bedrooms, two baths, and plenty of closets.

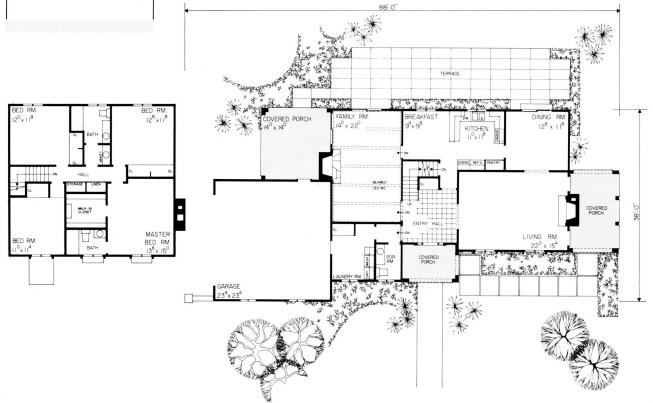

DESIGN A2376

1,422 sq. ft.—first floor
1,020 sq. ft.—second floor
38,134 cu. ft.

This board-and-batten house has all the country charm of a New England farmhouse. The large covered front porch will surely be appreciated during warm weather. Immediately off the front entrance is the corner living room. The dining room, with a bay window, can be easily served by the U-shaped kitchen. The family room has a raised-hearth fireplace, sliding glass doors to the rear terrace, and easy access to a work center, which is made up of a powder room, a laundry room, and a service entrance.

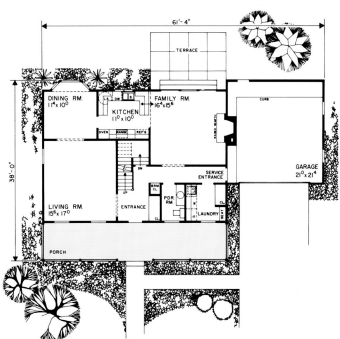

DESIGN A2776

1,134 sq. ft.—first floor
874 sq. ft.—second floor
31,600 cu. ft.

PORCHES 11

The long, low appearance of this traditional split-level home is accentuated by the large covered porch sheltering the bowed window and the inviting double front doors. Almost any exterior materials will work well on this finely proportioned home. The highlights of the interior include a large terrace off the family room, four bedrooms and three full baths, a beamed-ceiling family room, a sunken living room, a formal dining room, an informal breakfast room, an extra washroom, an outstanding kitchen, and two fireplaces.

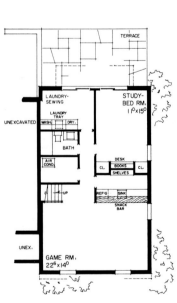

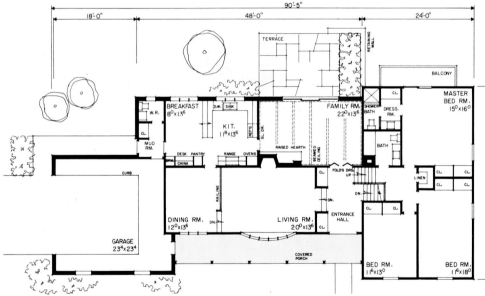

DESIGN A1927

1,272 sq. ft.—main level
960 sq. ft.—upper level
936 sq. ft.—lower level
36,815 cu. ft.

Here's a western ranch house
filled with wide, open spaces.
The full-length front porch is
covered, perfect for escaping
the sun during the day, or
for relaxing once the sun goes
down. To the rear of the
house, the front porch is
complemented by a full-
length terrace, with access
from every major room in
the house. This well-thought-
out design would suit a large,
active family.

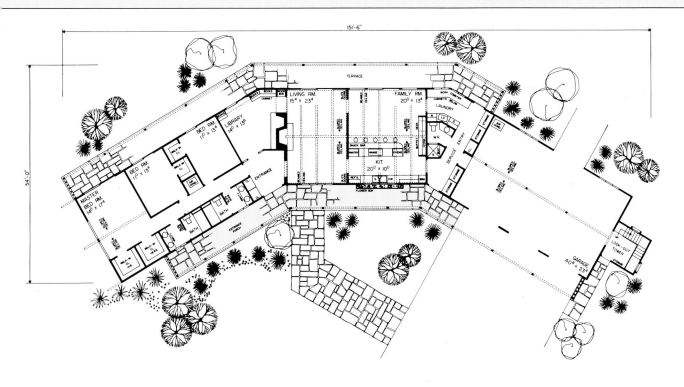

DESIGN A2258

2,504 sq. ft.
26,292 cu. ft.

PLANS FEATURING PORCHES

PORCHES 13

The two-story covered porch, supported by stately columns, gives this Colonial-style home an impressive facade. The plan features a full apartment to the side, for guests, relatives, or help. The main house has all the features to ensure a pleasant home environment for a lifetime. Note the terrace off the family room and breakfast nook for outdoor dining, and the handy three-car garage.

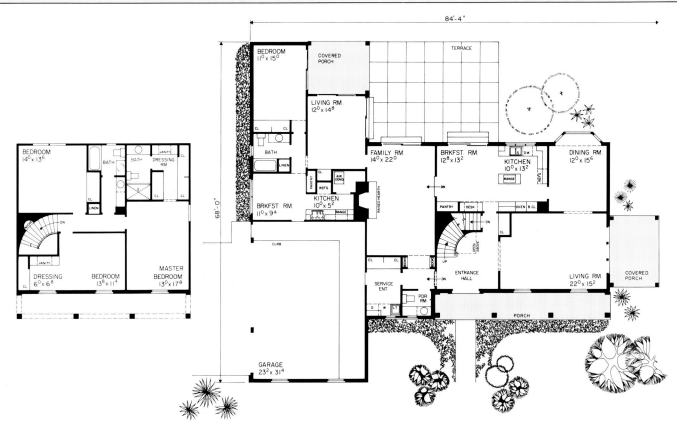

DESIGN A2762

2,345 sq. ft.—first floor
1,016 sq. ft.—second floor
53,740 cu. ft.

Classic good looks and fine proportions are the hallmark of this New England–style farmhouse. The large front porch invites family and friends to linger and enjoy the outdoors. There is also a back covered porch, accessible from the family room and close to the kitchen, just the place for outdoor meals. Both floors are efficiently laid out to make the most of available space. Note the study on the first floor, as well as the convenient laundry room and the convivial "tavern" in the family room. This house will be easy to enjoy.

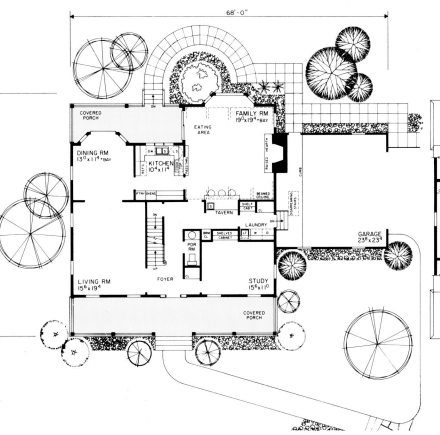

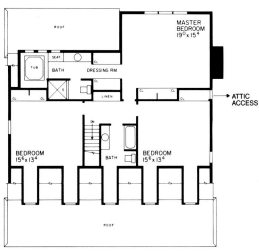

DESIGN A2890

1,612 sq. ft.—first floor
1,356 sq. ft.—second floor
47,010 cu. ft.

PLANS FEATURING PORCHES

PORCHES 15

The total square footage of this home is a mere 1,545 square feet, yet its features are many, including a front study, a powder room convenient to both kitchen and breakfast room, and a screened porch at the rear of the house. It has great exterior eye appeal, with horizontal lines, two second-story dormers, and traditional styling. Two bedrooms and two full baths are located on the second floor.

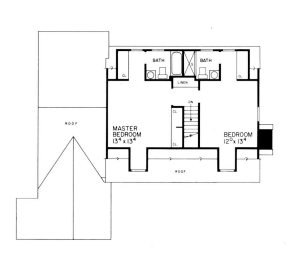

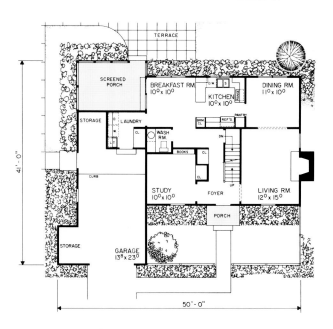

DESIGN A2655

893 sq. ft.—first floor
652 sq. ft.—second floor
22,555 cu. ft.

PORCHES 16

This is a farmhouse adaptation with all the up-to-date features of a new home, and the charm of such traditional features as a large wraparound front porch. The corner living room opens to the sizable dining room. This room will have plenty of natural light from the bay window overlooking the rear yard. Sliding glass doors to the rear terrace are practical attractions in both the sunken family room and the breakfast room. Recreational activities and hobbies can be pursued in the basement area. Four bedrooms and two baths are on the second floor.

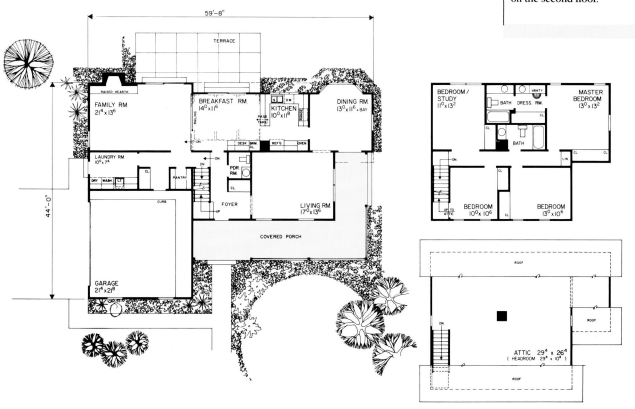

DESIGN A2774

1,370 sq. ft.—first floor
969 sq. ft.—second floor
38,305 cu. ft.

A Victorian home—even an updated version of one—wouldn't be complete without a porch. Here the porch wraps all the way around the house in a U-shape and is large enough to be considered as another room, especially pleasant for warm-weather outdoor activities. On close inspection of the plan you'll notice the second outside entrance with its own small covered porch. This door leads directly into the service area—convenient for everything from cleaning off muddy shoes to depositing grocery sacks. There's plenty of room and privacy for a large family in this three-story design. There are four bedrooms and a study on the second floor, and a fifth bedroom on the third floor, as well as a playroom and bathroom.

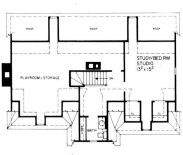

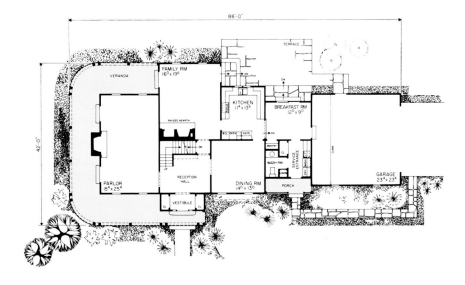

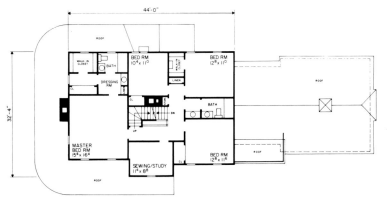

DESIGN A2645

1,600 sq. ft.—first floor
1,305 sq. ft.—second floor
925 sq. ft.—third floor
58,355 cu. ft.

A small covered porch provides entrance to this contemporary house. The unusual second-floor covered porch provides an enjoyable outdoor living area off three of the four upstairs bedrooms and gives the streetside facade a gracious appearance. To the rear of the house, there is a ground-level patio, and on the second floor, the master suite has a private sun deck—the perfect spot to get away from it all. The attached three-car garage is an unusual feature that would come in handy for a large family.

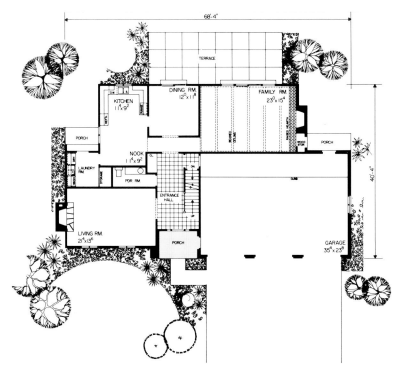

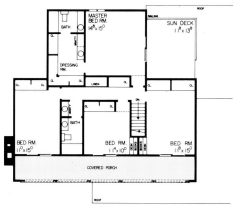

DESIGN A2388

1,441 sq. ft.—first floor
1,187 sq. ft.—second floor
36,466 cu. ft.

BALCONIES

IN YEARS PAST, balconies served as roof-protected but airy extensions of living space above the dust, heat, and noise of the streets. Today they perform the same function — and much more.

There is something about a balcony that appeals to the fanciful and romantic side of human nature. A balcony entices one outdoors to gaze at the view, encourages daydreaming, and invites putting up one's feet on the rail to contemplate the world away from the activity of the household and above the noise of the street. A small balcony off a bedroom conveys a sense of separateness and intimacy; a large one adjoining several rooms suggests sociability in a private setting. Because there is usually no way to reach a balcony except from inside the house, balconies also offer a hint of intrigue—a person on a balcony may be visible but beyond reach of those who pass beneath. A modern-day señorita can still step out on the balcony to flirt and be serenaded by a wishful suitor. No wonder balconies evoke such romantic notions!

Romantic as they may seem, balconies served an important function in Spain and in France in years past, and continue to be used today in many cultures. Houses were often situated directly on the thoroughfare, so first-floor windows and doors were small and kept barred or shuttered against the dust, heat, and noise. On the second story, however, windows gave way to doors opening directly to a balcony, shaded by the roof against the sun but admitting light and fresh air into the upper living quarters. Neighbors conversed above the crowds, and women and children could enjoy the outdoors in safety. At once private and friendly, balconies functioned as the outdoor living space of the day.

The balcony in early American houses acted in much the same way. In French and Spanish communities like New Orleans and Saint Augustine, the balcony usually spanned the length of the house under a deep roof overhang that provided plenty of shade. A number of French-style doors opened to the balcony to allow maximum circulation of people

On the balcony, you can be part of the scene below, or draw back into privacy if you wish.

and breezes to and from the main living areas located on the second floor. Sometimes the balcony continued around the entire upper story and doubled as a hallway. When it overlooked an inner courtyard, as in a number of Spanish designs, it was called a *loggia*; when it edged the building's outer walls, it was usually referred to as a *gallery*. In today's house designs, the balcony seldom wraps around the entire structure, but it remains a popular means of gaining private outdoor living space.

Because of its proximity to the interior room it serves, a balcony can give a special quality to the room itself. The addition of even a small balcony will make the smallest space seem bigger and more interesting. Larger, more public rooms, such as living and dining rooms, become gracious areas in which to entertain when they open to a balcony, especially if it affords a pleasant view. When the weather turns warm, few home features offer the attraction of a room in which the doors have been thrown open to a balcony.

Balconies come in all shapes and sizes, but the configuration is normally dictated by the depth of the roof overhang and the width of the house. A traditional balcony is fully covered by the main roof system and enclosed on three sides by a substantial rail. So designed, it can truly function as a self-contained "room," complete with indoor-outdoor furnishings and shade-loving plants. If the overhang of the main roof is too shallow to accommodate a fully covered balcony, the solution may be to create a living space that's a hybrid between deck and balcony, partially covered, partially open to the sky. Connecting a trellis to the edge of the eaves can extend the roof visually and give the impression of a traditional balcony.

Although the term *balcony* evokes mental pictures of Spanish Colonial designs, or the homes of New Orleans' French Quarter, any style house—from Swiss chalet to postmodern—can enjoy the pleasures of the balcony. As with decks, however, it is important that the balcony be in keeping with the proportions and style of the house itself. Railings can help integrate a balcony gracefully into the overall exterior appearance by underscoring the special features of a particular house style. As a rule, the traditional Spanish Colonial home carried a wood railing, or one simply cast from iron; French styles embellished their balconies with intricately patterned wrought iron. Today's house plans often echo details from the past but put them in a more modern context. A two-story stuccoed Spanish-style home of the 1980s might employ a wood or wrought-iron railing, or even enclose the balcony walls and finish them with stuc-

The combination of railing and wall allows an excellent view as well as protection, some privacy, and a sense of enclosure.

The balcony of this snow-covered Santa Fe adobe provides a perch to view the winter landscape. Like a traditional Spanish balcony, this one wraps around to run the length of the house. Unlike most balconies, however, this one has stairs.

co to make the balcony blend more harmoniously with the rest of the house and at the same time create a more private outdoor living space.

Balconies are ideal locations for planter boxes filled with hanging plants or flowers. Although the upkeep is somewhat demanding, these accessories lend a remarkable charm to the exterior of the house. Balconies overflowing with colorful flowers are a common feature of many European houses, and often one of the most memorable sights visitors take home with them. Another European custom is to give a small balcony more elbow room by attaching planter boxes to the outside of the railing. At the top of the rail, the boxes add a little height and extra privacy to the outdoor room; near the floor, they won't obstruct the distant view and can offer a border of color not unlike a flower bed.

Every outdoor living space benefits from places to sit and enjoy the weather and the garden. A large balcony can be segregated into distinct sitting areas, like a deck or a patio, and has the advantage of a roof canopy to protect furnishings from sun and rain. Small balconies feel more comfortable (and more romantic) with small-scale furnishings—a little table and a pair of chairs, cushioned benches along the house wall, or a loveseat oriented to take in the very best view.

1 *Spanning the back of the house and overlooking the courtyard, the balcony—with its generous roof overhang—provides shelter from the southwestern sun.*

2 *Open the French doors and step out on the balcony for a fabulous view, or stay inside and let the sounds and smells of the outdoors ride in on the breeze. Either way, the balcony enlarges the interior and beautifies the exterior.*

3 *An amazing vista of sea and sky and coast can be thoroughly appreciated from this balcony, where a narrow metal railing offers safety without sacrificing the view.*

1

2

3

BALCONIES

1

1 *Not all balconies have traditional balustrades. Partly enclosed by high and low walls, each of these balconies is a private and protected place—and the integrity of the southwestern style is honored.*

2 *Some balconies are purely ornamental. Reminiscent of a gallery—but with no doors leading on to it, and no sheltering roof—this one simply decorates. But it does this gloriously: sitting on top of the porch like a crown.*

3 *A contemporary house sports its own version of a traditional balcony. Shaded by the roof overhang, the streamlined balcony wraps around to take in the best view.*

2

3

PLANS FEATURING BALCONIES

BALCONIES 1

This comfortable, efficient four-bedroom home offers good traffic flow and access to balconies from three upstairs bedrooms. There's a breakfast room adjacent to the kitchen upstairs, plus a dining room and living room. An upper-level deck is also accessible from a rear entry. A bedroom-study downstairs opens onto a covered terrace. This house affords a great deal of outdoor living space in a variety of locations and exposures around the house.

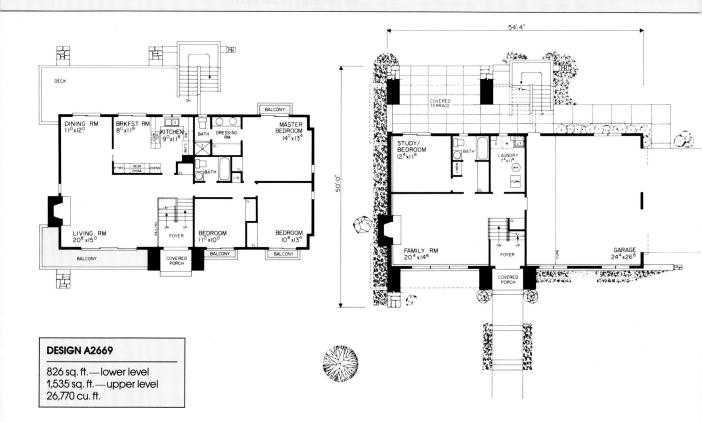

DESIGN A2669

826 sq. ft.—lower level
1,535 sq. ft.—upper level
26,770 cu. ft.

BALCONIES 2

This interesting contemporary house has a front balcony over the garage and entrance way, providing shelter as you walk to the front door. To the rear, there is a good-sized deck with stairs leading to two small terraces. With plenty of floor-to-ceiling windows and sliding glass doors, the interior of this house has an outdoor feeling. Both balcony and deck have specially contructed railings to harmonize with the exterior of the house and to allow built-in planting space for trailing plants.

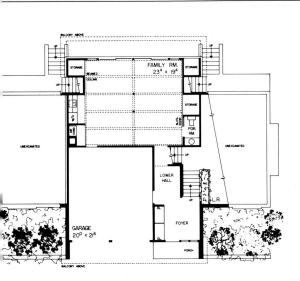

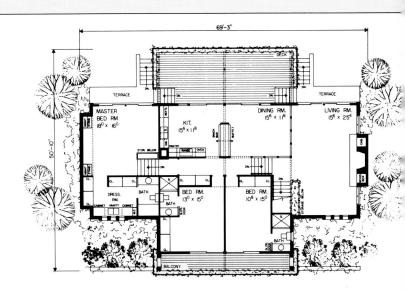

DESIGN A2247

1,049 sq. ft.—upper level
979 sq. ft.—middle levels
915 sq. ft.—lower level
29,880 cu. ft.

PLANS FEATURING BALCONIES

From the front of this traditional design, it appears that all of its living space is on one floor. The back of the house, however, reveals the tremendous amount of outdoor living space added to the plan as a result of exposing the lower level—all 1,344 square feet of it. The most popular spot in this hillside home might be the balcony, which runs the full length of the house. Then again, it could be the terrace adjacent to the family room on the lower level. Both terrace and balcony have a covered area to provide protection from the weather.

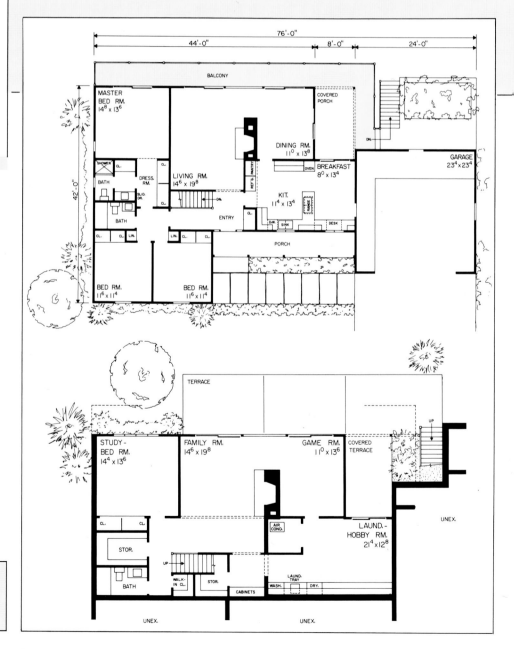

DESIGN A1974

1,680 sq. ft.—main level
1,344 sq. ft.—lower level
34,186 cu. ft.

BALCONIES 4

This large Spanish-style hacienda has over 5,000 square feet of living area, excluding the garage. Measuring over 100 feet across the front, with full-length second-floor balcony, this design gives the impression of a cluster of units—almost like a small village. For outdoor living, in addition to the large balcony there is an intimate courtyard garden and covered porch accessible from the downstairs bedroom, as well as a screened-in porch off the living room and breakfast nook. There are five bedrooms on the second floor, plus a sixth bedroom and a study on the first floor. The master bedroom features two full baths and a sleeping porch, ideal for a warm climate. The 18-foot dining room will accommodate large dinner parties. This is a great house for large, active families.

DESIGN A2214

3,011 sq. ft.—first floor
2,297 sq. ft.—second floor
78,585 cu. ft.

BALCONIES 5

This traditionally styled hillside home has two distinctively different facades. From the front, two formal double doors open to a spacious center entry, which routes traffic to both levels of the house. To the rear, there are two balconies, a large second-story deck, and two terraces—ample space to enjoy the pleasures of outdoor living. Note the two fireplaces, the two studies, the two large living areas, and the two kitchens—one on the lower level for use during summer.

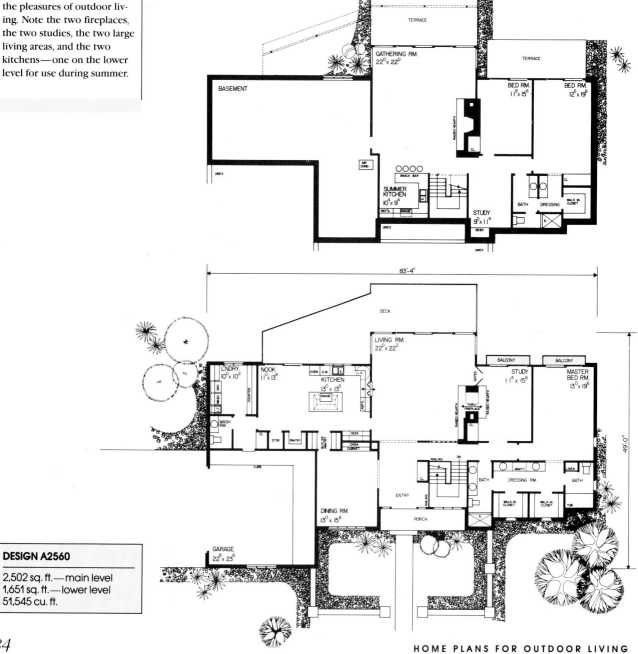

DESIGN A2560

2,502 sq. ft.—main level
1,651 sq. ft.—lower level
51,545 cu. ft.

This Spanish Colonial home features the traditional second-floor covered balcony. An essential element of this style, the balcony also provides cover for the entrance porch below. The exterior may reflect a bygone era, but its floor plan offers all of today's conveniences. French doors open off the family room onto the front porch, and the large rear terrace is reached by sliding glass doors in the breakfast room.

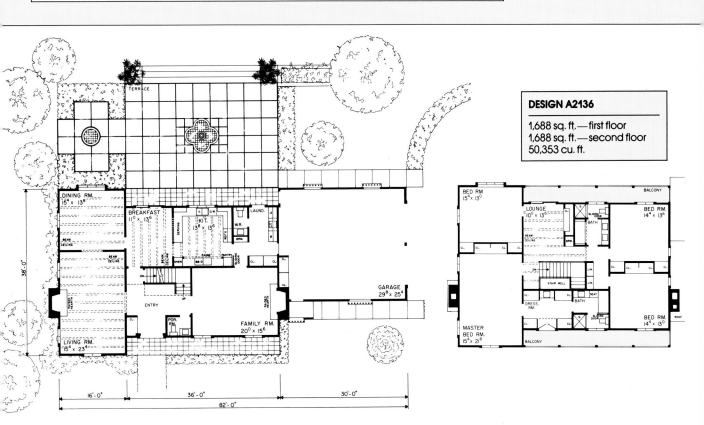

DESIGN A2136

1,688 sq. ft.—first floor
1,688 sq. ft.—second floor
50,353 cu. ft.

PLANS FEATURING BALCONIES

BALCONIES 7

With five balconies and three terraces, this house has plenty of outdoor space for all members of the family. These unique balconies add great beauty to the exterior. The rear terrace is reached by sliding glass doors from the lower-level bedroom and activity room. The side terrace functions with the activity-family room area. This home has a good deal of interior space as well. Take note of the size of the gathering room, family room, and activity room. There's also a large dining room and four bedrooms.

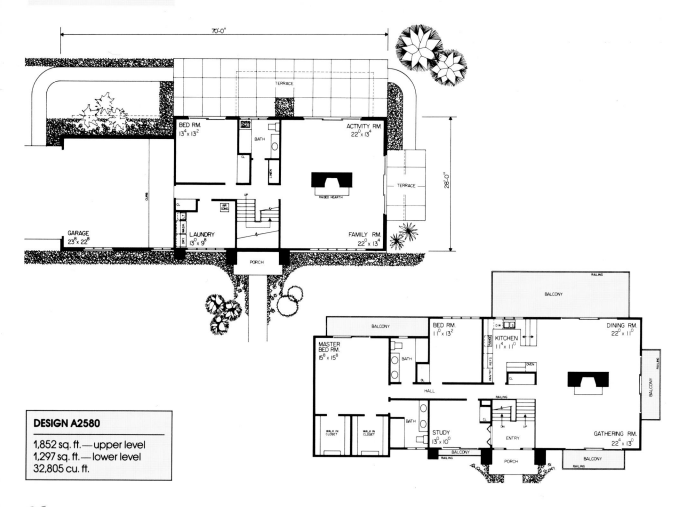

DESIGN A2580

1,852 sq. ft.—upper level
1,297 sq. ft.—lower level
32,805 cu. ft.

BALCONIES 8

Every room in this large family house opens onto a terrace, a deck, or a balcony— sometimes more than one! Indoor-outdoor living will be enjoyed to the maximum with this unique plan. Features include a huge gathering room with a raised-hearth fireplace in the center, sloped ceilings, and separate areas for dining and games. A family room on the lower level, of equal size to the gathering room, has its own center fireplace and adjoining terrace. There is an efficient kitchen and a dining nook with a built-in desk. The master suite has a private balcony.

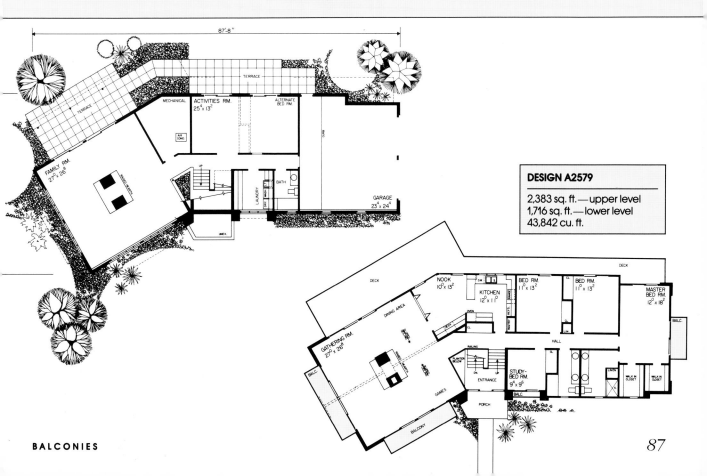

DESIGN A2579

2,383 sq. ft.—upper level
1,716 sq. ft.—lower level
43,842 cu. ft.

BALCONIES 9

This house makes it easy to enjoy the outdoors. The contemporary-style design projects a solid streetside exterior but is open to the rear by means of a very large balcony and a lower-level terrace. The dining room, gathering room, study, and master bedroom all have access, via sliding glass doors, to the balcony. Downstairs, the terrace or patio can be reached from two bedrooms and the large activity room. The plan also includes a formal dining room, a kitchen for people who love to cook, and fireplaces on both floors.

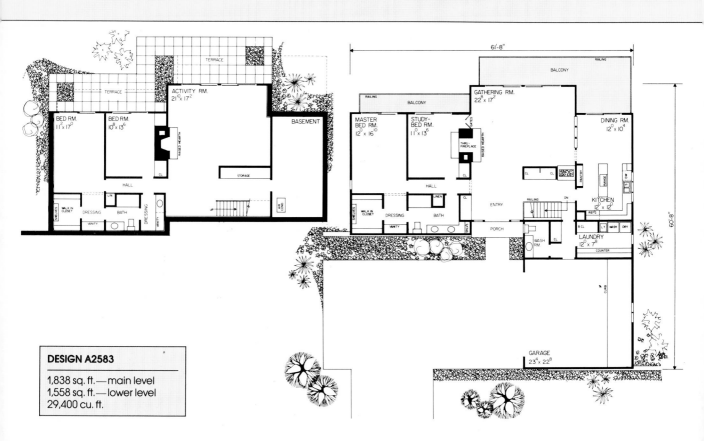

DESIGN A2583

1,838 sq. ft.—main level
1,558 sq. ft.—lower level
29,400 cu. ft.

This contemporary house with an adaptation of a mansard roof is ideal for a narrow hillside lot. The front of the house is shielded from the street by the garage and an enclosed entrance court. The rear of the house opens up to a large second-floor balcony, accessible from both the living and dining rooms via three sets of sliding doors and a first-floor terrace available for use by the downstairs bedrooms. The living-dining area has a raised-hearth fireplace. The open staircase to the lower level has a dramatic view of the planting area below. Note the over-sized garage for extra storage.

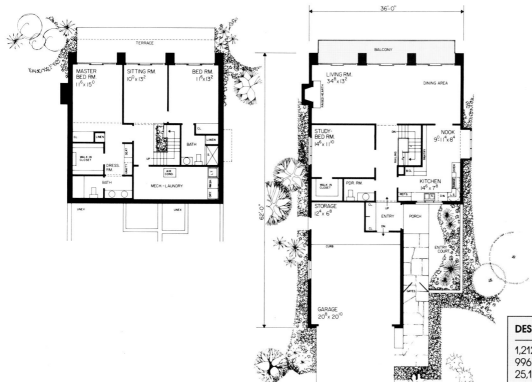

DESIGN A2725

1,212 sq. ft.—main level
996 sq. ft.—lower level
25,120 cu. ft.

BALCONIES 11

This narrow dramatic 42-foot-wide house can be built on a narrow lot to cut down on overall costs. The projecting front garage creates a pleasing curved driveway, ideal for a variety of landscape treatments. The rear balcony stretching across the entire length of the house offers three of the four bedrooms a protected outdoor living space. Below, there is a ground-level terrace off the family dining room and living room, partially shaded by the balcony and enclosed by extensions of the house walls. The entrance-level foyer is reached through the covered porch. Stairs lead down to the living room, family room, kitchen and dining area, and up to the four bedroom, two-bath sleeping area.

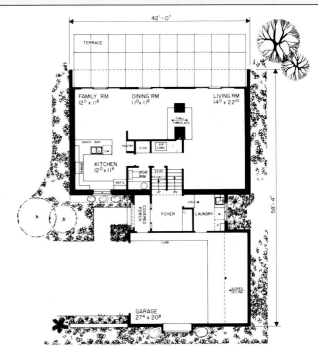

DESIGN A2842

156 sq. ft.—entrance level
1,040 sq. ft.—upper level
1,022 sq. ft.—lower level
25,630 cu. ft.

BALCONIES 12

The rustic nature of this split-level home is highlighted by the rough-textured stone, natural-toned wood siding, and the wide overhanging roof with exposed beams. This house is perfect for wooded settings because of the views and outdoor access provided by the large upper-level balcony and lower-level terrace. The upper balcony is accessible from the master bedroom, the family room, and the dining room. The lower terrace provides access to the study and the game and hobby room, making it ideal for indoor-outdoor entertaining.

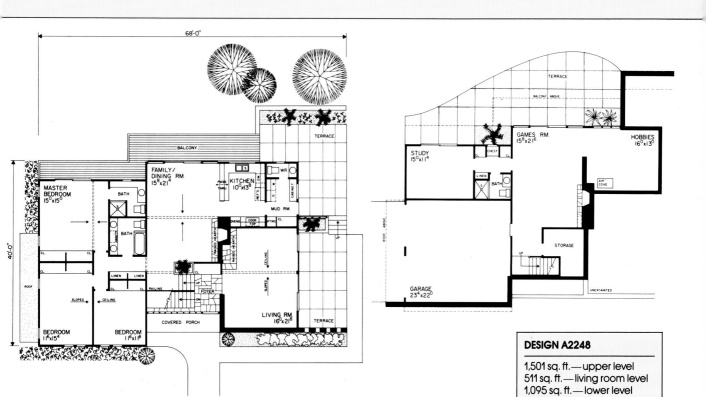

DESIGN A2248

1,501 sq. ft.—upper level
511 sq. ft.—living room level
1,095 sq. ft.—lower level
30,486 cu. ft.

BALCONIES 13

Here is an economical home that can be constructed with either of two exteriors, one of which is illustrated here. Its upstairs, nonfunctional balcony lends a gracious touch to the house, while the rear terrace provides convenient space for a variety of outdoor activities off the dining room, kitchen, and breakfast nook. The two study areas, one on each floor, provide plenty of mutipurpose informal living space.

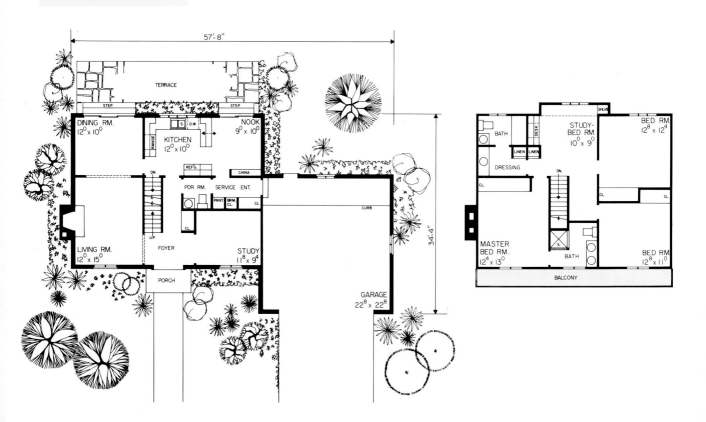

DESIGN A2525

919 sq. ft.—first floor
1,019 sq. ft.—second floor
29,200 cu. ft.

A re-creation of the New Orleans style, this house is highlighted by a second-floor balcony with typical wrought-iron railing and posts, plus two sets of French doors. The balcony is accessible from two of the five upstairs bedrooms, including the master suite. A good-sized covered porch off the living room leads to the large semi-circular terrace. Note the functional floor plan, with a workshop and laundry room off the garage, and two fireplaces—one in the family room and one in the living room.

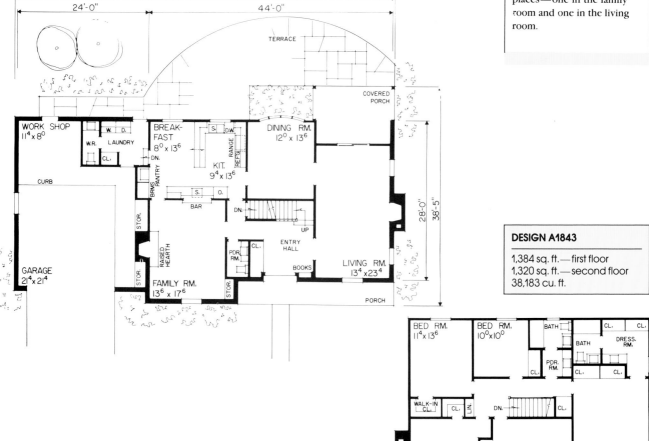

DESIGN A1843

1,384 sq. ft.—first floor
1,320 sq. ft.—second floor
38,183 cu. ft.

BALCONIES 15

This house, which could also be used as mountain vacation home, has an outdoor deck, a balcony, and a covered first-floor terrace. The railings around the deck and balcony lend a Swiss-chalet-style charm to the exterior. There are two fireplaces and a huge L-shaped living and dining room area. There are three good-sized bedrooms. Note the ski lounge and the wet hall for skis—practical features for a winter retreat.

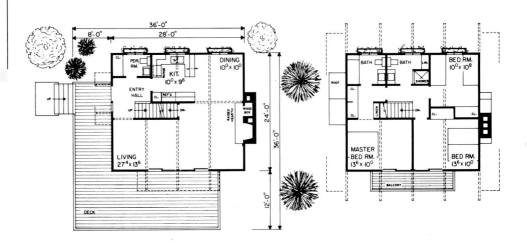

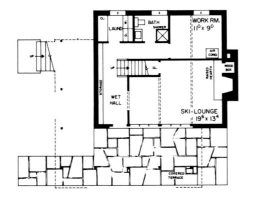

DESIGN A2429

672 sq. ft.—main level
672 sq. ft.—upper level
672 sq. ft.—lower level
19,152 cu. ft.

This Southern Colonial adaptation has a truly distinctive facade. The balconies on two sides of the house provide delightful outdoor living space off the upstairs bedrooms. The solidly proportioned pillars of the porticos lend an air of dignity to the house, while the central entry opens to a formal interior planned to assure each room a full measure of privacy. If desired, however, the family room may be easily opened up to the kitchen–breakfast-nook area. The library can be used as a quiet retreat. The attached garage has a generous storage area, ideal for garden and lawn equipment.

73'-10"

81'-8"

GARAGE
23⁴ x 23⁴

STORAGE
12⁰ x 6⁰

TERRACE

DINING RM.
12⁰ x 17⁶

KITCHEN
11⁰ x 11⁰

NOOK
10⁰ x 11⁰

FAMILY RM.
15⁰ x 17⁶

PORTICO

LAUNDRY

POR.
RM.

DESK
SHELVES

LIVING RM.
19⁴ x 17⁶

ENTRY

LIBRARY
19⁴ x 11⁰

PORTICO

ROOF

BED RM.
15⁰ x 15⁰

BED RM.
12⁰ x 11⁴

BATH

SEAT

STEP

DRESSING
RM.

BALCONY

LINEN LINEN

WALK IN
CLOSET

WALK IN
CLOSET

BATH

WALK IN
CLOSET

BATH

CL

CL

BED RM.
19⁴ x 14⁶

HALL

MASTER
BED RM.
19⁴ x 17⁶

BALCONY

DESIGN A2336

1,872 sq. ft.—first floor
1,872 sq. ft.—second floor
65,503 cu. ft.

COURTYARDS
& ATRIUMS

ENCLOSED BY WALLS but open to the sky, courtyards and atriums can offer near-total privacy sometimes hard to find in other outdoor areas. They also lend themselves beautifully to gardening on a small scale.

For as long as there have been houses and gardens, there have been courtyards—garden areas enclosed by the walls of a house. The patio of ancient times was a form of courtyard, usually encompassing a garden and places to relax, and also practically equipped for cooking, dining, and day-to-day living. In the temperate Mediterranean countries, the garden courtyard blossomed as an integral part of home design, with fountains and furnishings sharing the private outside space with flower beds and citrus trees. In warmer, more arid regions, it served as a retreat from the hot sun and drying winds—an oasis of shade, protected by walls and overhangs. By medieval times the idea of the courtyard had traveled north and west into Europe, and from there to the New World. Many early American builders incorporated courtyards into their houses, and home planners today continue to include this private and versatile indoor-outdoor living space in their designs.

A stepping-stone pathway meanders from the courtyard gate past a garden seat—a quiet place to stop for a moment's relaxation.

A traditional courtyard is square or rectangular in shape, enclosed by the walls of the house itself or by a combination of walls and fences. Although the courtyards of earlier times were often large in size—sometimes big enough to accommodate a wagon and a team of horses—courtyards today tend to be smaller, more intimate spaces, usually no larger than a quarter of the total floor area of the house. A courtyard doesn't have to be completely enclosed on all four sides, but at least three walls or fences are necessary to maintain the feeling of privacy and enclosure.

Although courtyards are typically situated at the center of the plan, surrounded by the "U" configuration of the house, they sometimes appear at the side or the rear. They may also lie near the front entrance, or serve as the entrance itself, a kind of outdoor foyer. Entrance courtyards function as a well-defined transition area between the public arena—the street or the outer yard—and the private spaces of the house. As a prelude to the private world within, an entrance courtyard should receive the same care and attention as an interior room. Plantings and furnishings should offer a reflection of the owners and their home—the mood one of welcome.

Like the courtyard, the atrium has evolved as an indoor-outdoor living space, but its original function was somewhat different. In Roman architecture the atrium was the principal living room, central to the religious and domestic life of the family. It was located in the center of the house, its roof open to the sky and its walls formed by the surrounding rooms. Usually a colonnade edged the square or rectangular atrium, protecting the interior and serving as a covered hallway. The open-air atrium had furnishings, sculpture, an altar dedicated to the gods, and, as a focal point, a large sunken pool with a fountain—aesthetically pleasing to the senses and functionally designed to catch rainwater for household use.

A modern atrium too can serve as a principal living room year-round, especially when covered with glass or fiberglass to protect the area from inclement weather. In many ways an open-air atrium acts as a central courtyard, ideal for fair-weather sitting, dining, and gardening, and accessible from the surrounding rooms through sliding glass or French doors. By its very nature, however, the open-air atrium must be engineered to accept rainwater—perhaps even snow—with careful thought to adequate drainage and the type of floor surface.

The covered atrium is popular in regions where rains are frequent and winters harsh. A glass-covered atrium that is also walled in by the house makes a perfect spot for raising tropical plants any time of the year and provides an excellent source of warmth and humidity in winter months. In summer, though, a covered atrium can become too hot and humid to enjoy without proper ventilation. A roof covering that slides back, skylights that can be opened, or a wall-mounted exhaust fan that vents to the outside can make a big difference.

Another version of the covered atrium incorporates this area directly into the house interior, defining its "walls" with a change in floor level and/or a partial wall, and covered by a transparent roof that floods the atrium and surrounding spaces with natural light. A sunken-garden living room with a fountain at its heart, a light-filled breakfast nook enclosed by partial walls, or a glass-roofed entry hall fragrant with the scent of orchids—these are indoor rooms with an outdoor personality.

Such enclosed indoor-outdoor areas lend themselves to gardening in a variety of ways without making the owner a slave to the garden. A courtyard enclosed by even three walls enjoys a microclimate more moderate than that of the nearby outdoors—often experiencing reduced winds, less intense sun, and fewer extremes of hot and cold. In a courtyard, where a masonry floor typically sits right on the ground, the garden can be designed to incorporate a wide variety of trees, shrubs, and flowers. Most atriums, however, rest on the same foundation as the house, and require that planting beds be designed with proper attention to such factors as drainage, distribution of weight, size of mature plants, and potentially extensive root systems. If beds are not feasible, almost any plant can be grown in containers, including large palms and tree ferns. Either way, a faucet close at hand simplifies watering. Atrium flooring should be constructed of material that can withstand the wear and tear of gardening—concrete, brick, flagstone, and tile can all be used successfully.

In the tradition of Rome and the whole Mediterranean region, fountains and small pools add a touch of magic to the courtyard or atrium. However, a house does not have to be "Mediterranean" in design to accept an atrium or courtyard fountain as its focal point.

With plantings, a fountain, and some well-positioned seating, such an indoor-outdoor enclosure can become the most popular area of the house—for morning coffee or an evening glass of wine, for weekend brunch or an impromptu barbecue, for solitary sitting or lively conversation. A courtyard in particular makes an excellent play yard for children and pets, and an ideal space for sunning or relaxing in privacy. Finally, a courtyard or atrium can be the perfect solution for a small or problem lot where outdoor living space offers little privacy from neighbors, where the house sits directly on a busy street, or where the site itself is ill-suited to a patio or terrace design.

A fountain plays in a formal pool—the heart of the traditional courtyard. Classical and Renaissance influences show in the stone inlay and the shape of the pool.

1 *A courtyard makes an effective entrance way by providing a space between private and public domains. Low walls give definition without a sense of confinement.*

1

2 *Higher walls ensure more privacy but still allow a glimpse of the beyond. The courtyard has a roomlike feeling, conducive to family activity. Container plants trim the ledges, which are low enough to make watering easy.*

3 *The formal entrance court invites the visitor while protecting the family's privacy. Traversing a sedate garden hedged with box-wood, a brick walk leads up to a wrought-iron gate—a traditional feature of Spanish-style homes. Beyond, the intimate little court is shaded and screened by flowering growth. An orna-mental balcony—just wide enough for a few small plants—echoes the grillwork of the gate.*

2

3

4

4 *A small courtyard with a few special touches—like an arbor-covered gate—can become a magical place.*

1

2

3

1 *This southwestern atrium has a lot in common with its ancient Roman ancestor: it is open to the sky, defined by the outer walls of the surrounding rooms, and bordered by a covered colonnade.*

2 *With glass walls, an open-air atrium gives pleasure inside or out.*

3 *Completely integrated into the house, this covered atrium is defined by a lattice-like structure on one side and a colonnade on the other. Brickwork edges the central planting area, picking up the rich tones of adjacent wood and tile floors.*

4 *Decidedly modern, this atrium still performs its traditional functions. Centrally located, it is easily accessible; open above but enclosed by the house, it is airy and private; spacious, it can accommodate all sorts of activity—not the least of which is enjoying the architecture and the patterns of shadow and light it produces.*

4

COURTYARDS 1

For something different, consider this L-shaped ranch house adapted from old Spanish designs. The house is entered through an arch with wrought-iron gates, which leads immediately to a private courtyard entrance garden— cool, calm, and removed from the street. All the major rooms function through sliding glass doors to the three terraces beyond. The interior has a feeling of spaciousness, with large expanses of glass and a sloping ceiling. The open living area makes for easy entertaining.

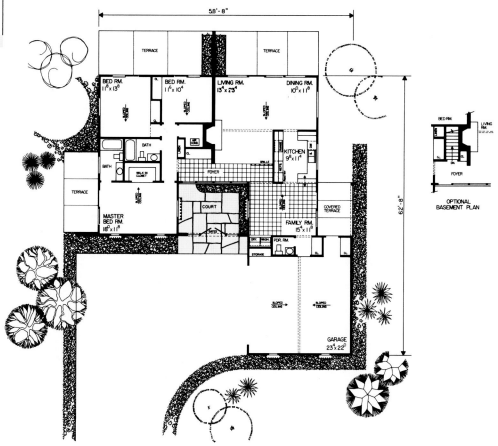

DESIGN A2200

1,695 sq. ft.
18,916 cu. ft.

COURTYARDS 2

Outdoor family living is provided by this distinctive Tudor adaptation. The completely enclosed entrance court is not only attractive, it is also an ideal environment for young children. There are two large terraces to the rear and the side of the house, providing plenty of outdoor space for entertaining, relaxing, or dining. There are four bedrooms, two downstairs and two up, as well as a second-floor playroom, a study or sewing room, and four full baths and an extra washroom.

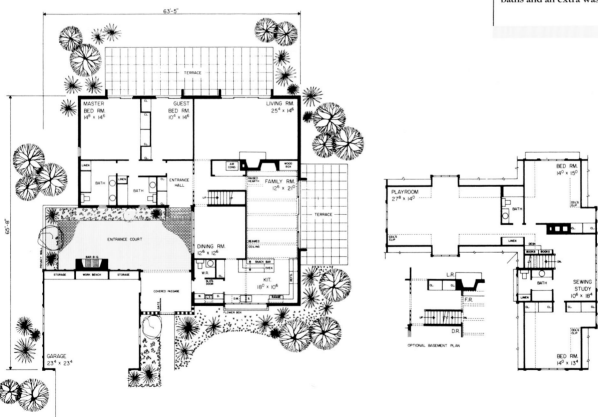

DESIGN A2274

1,941 sq. ft.—first floor
1,392 sq. ft.—second floor
32,580 cu. ft.

PLANS FEATURING COURTYARDS

Here is a western ranch house with an authentic Spanish flavor. Across the front, arched walls provide an interesting backdrop for the long raised planter. Entrance to the house is through a large interior courtyard, filled with plants and featuring a fountain. There are two large terraces, one wrapping around the side of the house, and a private terrace adjoining two of the four bedrooms. The low-pitched tile roof features a wide overhang with exposed rafter tails.

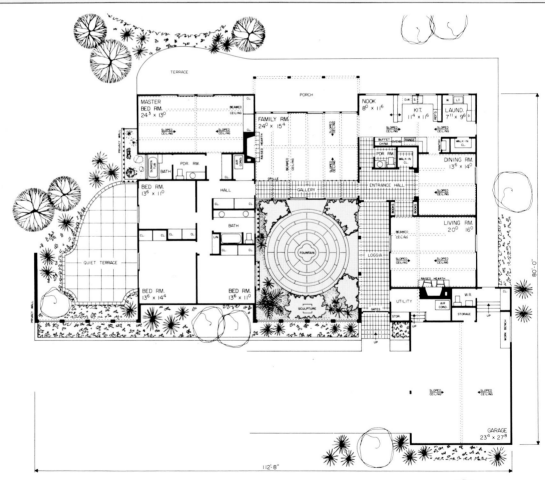

DESIGN A2294

3,056 sq. ft.
34,533 cu. ft.

COURTYARDS 4

The charm of the old Spanish Southwest is captured in this design. The large private entrance court is an attractive and welcoming space. The family, dining, and living rooms will cater to the family's varied group activities. Four bedrooms and a sewing room are on the second floor. The sewing room can be turned into a fifth bedroom.

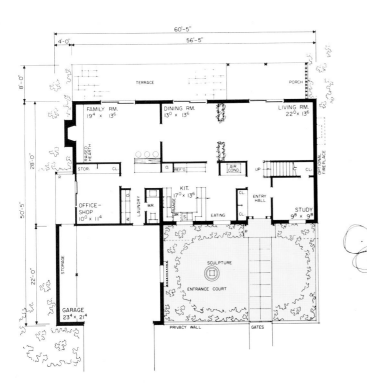

DESIGN A1753

1,580 sq. ft.—first floor
1,008 sq. ft.—second floor
26,484 cu. ft.

PLANS FEATURING COURTYARDS

COURTYARDS 5

The formal facade of this mansard-roofed house hides a variety of pleasures. On the other side of the entrance gates lies a formal courtyard, complete with center fountain, patio area, and enough room for a garden. Every room in the house looks out onto this courtyard, and there are windows on the sides of the house as well. In addition to the courtyard, there is a terrace off the family room at the rear of the house. There are four bedrooms, a formal dining room, and an efficient kitchen with a breakfast room.

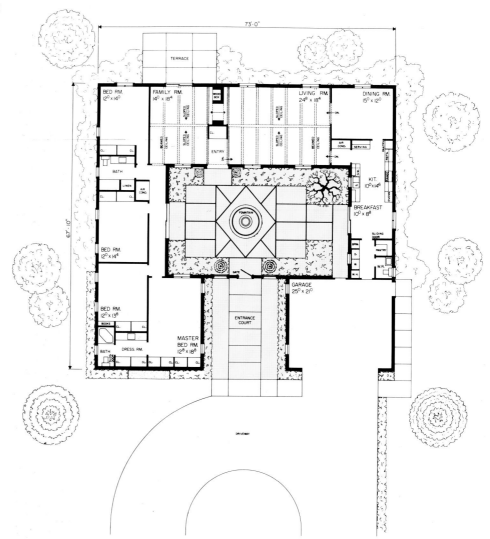

DESIGN A2177

2,802 sq. ft.
34,133 cu. ft.

A walled courtyard with a reflecting pool and raised planters is a gracious way to enter this one-story Spanish-style home. The Spanish theme is accented by the grillwork and the tile roof. There is a large patio to the rear of the house, accessible from both the master bedroom and family room. The front living room has sliding glass doors that open to the entrance court; the adjacent dining room features a bay window. Four bedrooms are in the sleeping wing of the house.

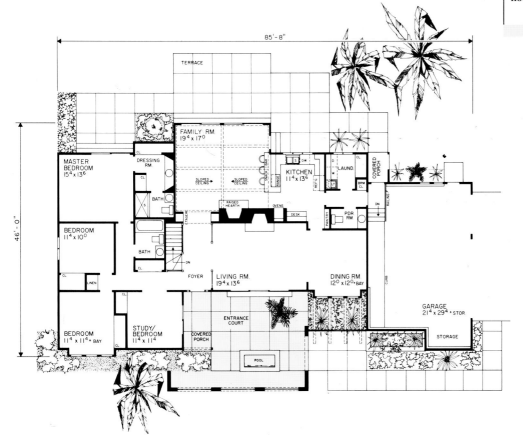

DESIGN A2820

2,261 sq. ft.
46,830 cu. ft.

PLANS FEATURING COURTYARDS

COURTYARDS 7

An enclosed courtyard sets this home apart. The dining room and two of the four bedrooms open onto this pleasant outdoor space by means of large windows or sliding glass doors. Other unusual features include the large keeping room, complete with a wet bar, a built-in bookcase, and a fireplace-woodbox combination, plus sliding glass doors to the terrace beyond. This design provides plenty of space for family life as well as indoor-outdoor entertaining.

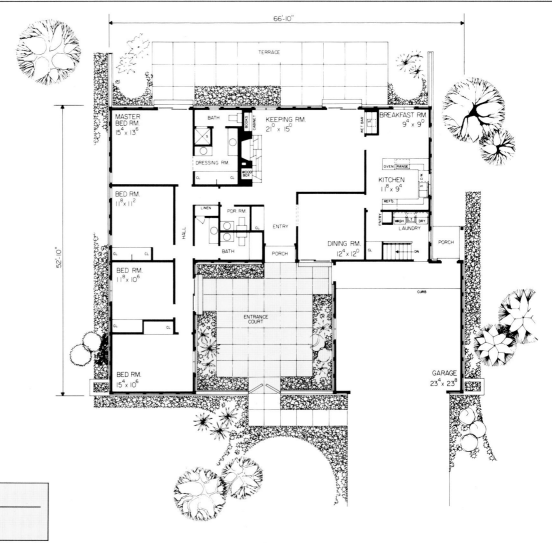

DESIGN A2620

2,048 sq. ft.
42,000 cu. ft.

Here is a unique, brick-veneer traditional home with a completely surrounded entrance court. The covered front porch, with its well-proportioned columns, provides extra shelter for the covered walkway to the court and an impressive approach to the double front doors. Glass panels open onto the planting areas from inside. The configuration of this house creates interesting roof planes. The interior features include two fireplaces, plenty of closets, two full baths plus a powder room, beamed ceilings in the family room, a snack bar with a pass-through to the efficient kitchen, a utility room, and interior planting units. The recessed rear terrace is accessible through sliding glass doors from the four major rooms: family, living, dining, and master bedroom.

64'-10"

66'-5"

TERRACE

FAMILY RM.
13⁴ x 19⁰

MASTER
BED RM.
13⁴ x 14⁸

BEAMED
CEILING

DINING RM.
12⁰ x 10⁸

LIVING RM.
17⁴ x 14⁰

DRESSING RM.

BATH

SNACK BAR

CL

CL

W.B.

FOYER

LINEN

CL

KITCHEN
13⁴ x 10⁴

CL

CL

BED RM.
13⁴ x 10⁰

RANGE

PDR.
RM.

BATH

DRY WASH PANTRY

UTILITY RM.
13⁴ x 6⁰

AIR
COND.

ENTRANCE
COURT

CL

CL

STORAGE

GATES

GARAGE
21⁴ x 21⁴

BED RM.
11⁴ x 13⁴

BED RM.
11⁴ x 13⁴

CL

PORCH

DESIGN A2371

2,389 sq. ft.
29,220 cu. ft.

COURTYARDS 9

The brick-walled entrance court sets a formal tone for this traditional home. At the front of the house, all the rooms can take advantage of the views offered by this private space complete with a fountain. To the rear of the house, all the main rooms have sliding glass doors to the terrace. They are away from the confusion of the work center, yet easily accessible. A study and a separate office are also available. Four bedrooms are on the second floor.

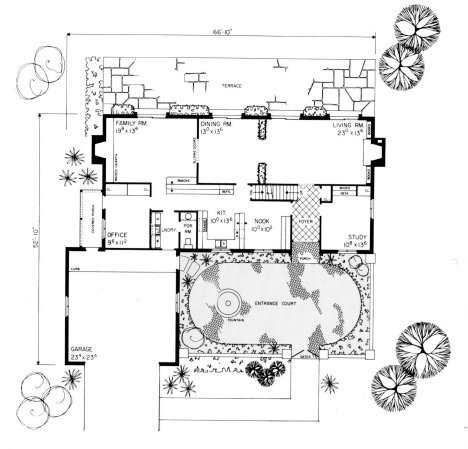

DESIGN A2326

1,674 sq. ft. — first floor
1,107 sq. ft. — second floor
53,250 cu. ft.

COURTYARDS 10

The regal character of this home is enhanced by the classic symmetry of the front facade and the distinctive raised terrace. The recessed front entrance shelters paneled double doors opening to a formal hall. The rear courtyard is enclosed by the walls of the house on three sides to assure privacy, and is accessible from the master bedroom and the family room through sliding glass doors. Separating the formal living and dining rooms are finely proportioned round wood columns.

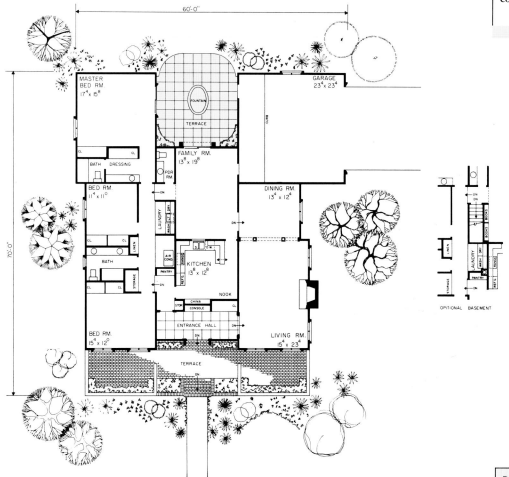

DESIGN A2347

2,322 sq. ft.
26,572 cu. ft.

COURTYARDS 11

This distinctive design may look like it belongs in a warm climate, but wherever it is built, this home will offer much in the way of easy indoor-outdoor living. The central core is made up of the living, dining, and family rooms, plus the kitchen. Each functions with an outdoor living area, including an enclosed entrance court and large side courtyard. The younger generation has a separate sleeping zone. The attached garage provides direct access to front entry.

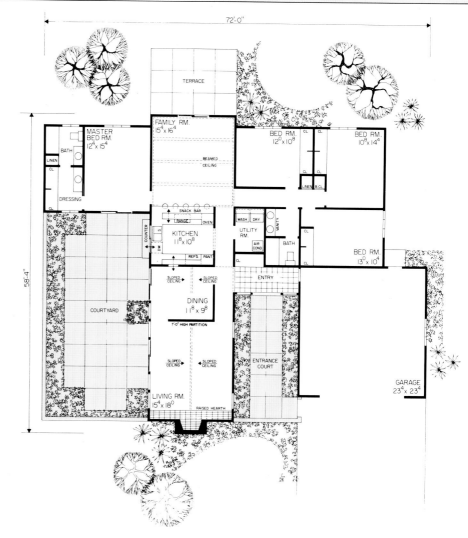

DESIGN A2386

1,994 sq. ft.
22,160 cu. ft.

COURTYARDS 12

A unique adaptation of an early American farmhouse, this design features an interesting entrance court that is partially shielded from the street. Its covered walkway offers protection from inclement weather and provides a shaded, cool environment for both plants and people. A large curved terrace in the rear is accessible from both the family room and the master bedroom. Note the stylish chimney design and the bookcase-lined alcove in the living room, complete with a woodbox that doubles as a seat.

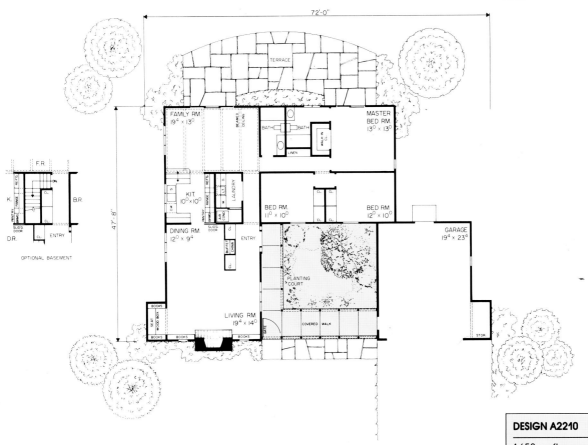

DESIGN A2210

1,658 sq. ft.
22,804 cu. ft.

PLANS FEATURING COURTYARDS

COURTYARDS 13

Reminiscent of the West, this home is luxurious in both its appearance and its livability. The rambling ranch house encloses a dramatic entrance court, complete with a central fountain. Additional outdoor living space is amply provided by two private terraces, a large living terrace, and an even larger patio surrounding the pool and cabaña. Three bedrooms, plus a master suite with a dressing room and bath, form a private bedroom wing. Formal and informal living areas serve ideally for all types of entertaining.

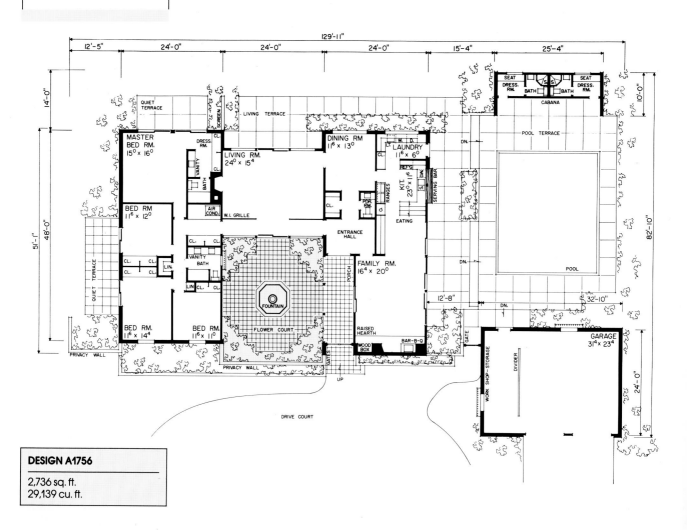

DESIGN A1756

2,736 sq. ft.
29,139 cu. ft.

COURTYARDS 14

This four-bedroom home features front and rear enclosed courtyards. The great room takes full advantage of both, with two sets of sliding glass doors—perfect for warm-weather entertaining. Family features include a built-in wet bar and fireplace. Note the conveniently located mudroom next to the garage, the built-in china cabinets in the breakfast room, and the adjoining terrace.

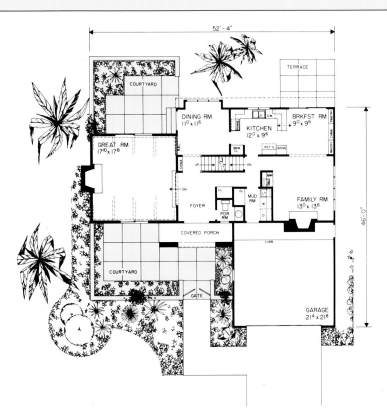

DESIGN A2801

1,172 sq. ft.—first floor
884 sq. ft.—second floor
32,510 cu. ft.

COURTYARDS 15

An attractive contemporary design with traditional touches. This house is entered through two columns, complete with a wrought-iron gate, leading to a private entrance court with plenty of space for plants. In addition to the entrance court, there is a total of four terraces and a balcony. Note the outstanding master bedroom with two baths—each with a large walk-in closet—sliding glass doors to a private side terrace, and an adjacent study. This configuration allows for total privacy for both parents and children. Entertaining will be easy in the gathering room, with its large fireplace and attractive balcony, accessible through two sliding glass doors. The U-shaped kitchen utilizes a triangular work pattern, thought to be the most efficient.

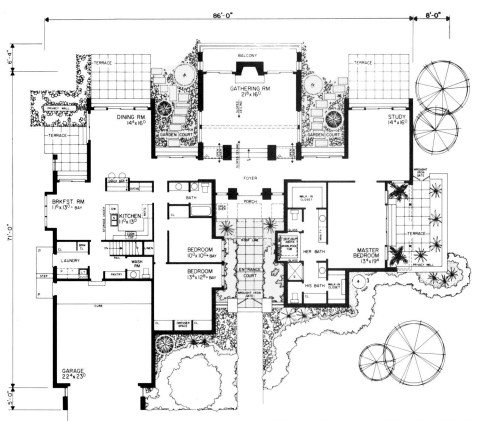

DESIGN A2857

2,982 sq. ft.
60,930 cu. ft.

A centrally located interior atrium is one of the most interesting features of this contemporary Spanish-style home. The atrium has a built-in seat and will bring light to the adjacent living, dining, and breakfast rooms. Beyond the foyer, sunken one step, is a tiled reception hall that includes a powder room. This area leads to the sleeping wing and up one step to the family room. Overlooking the family room is a 279-square-foot railed lounge that can be used for a variety of family activities. The columned rear terrace provides partial over-head shelter and not only adds distinction to the rear of the house, but is ideal for warm-weather entertaining.

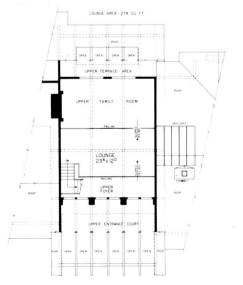

DESIGN A2670

3,058 sq. ft.
44,210 cu. ft.

PLANS FEATURING ATRIUMS

ATRIUMS 2

This spacious home offers the residents many options for enjoying the outdoors. Main level rooms offer large glass windows and/or balconies for viewing the outdoors. Three lower-level rooms offer direct access to terraces. These two levels are tied together by a centrally located skylighted atrium that functions as a thoroughfare between the different levels and brings light into the center of this large house. The center skylight panels are hinged and motor-operated for ventilation. It is also equipped with a summer sun shade.

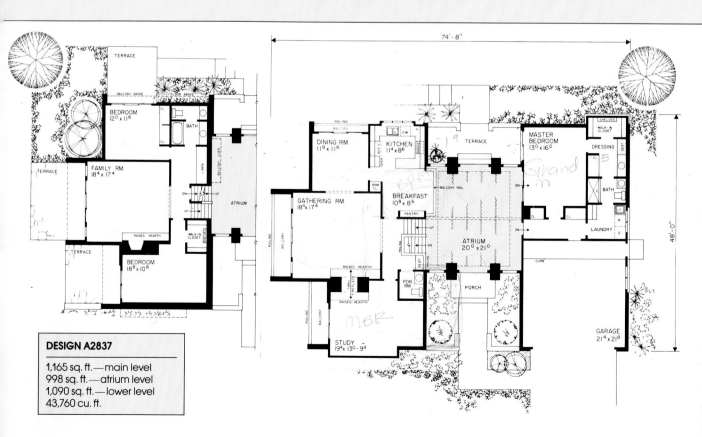

DESIGN A2837

1,165 sq. ft.—main level
998 sq. ft.—atrium level
1,090 sq. ft.—lower level
43,760 cu. ft.

ATRIUMS 3

Unique to this plan is the entrance atrium. This house allows for a variety of energy-saving passive solar features to be incorporated into its design. Multiple plot plans (included with the blue-prints) illustrate which eleva-tions should be solarized for different sites and how extra features can be added, including such options as attaching a greenhouse to the family room, turning the back porch into a solarium, and adding skylights over the entrance atrium.

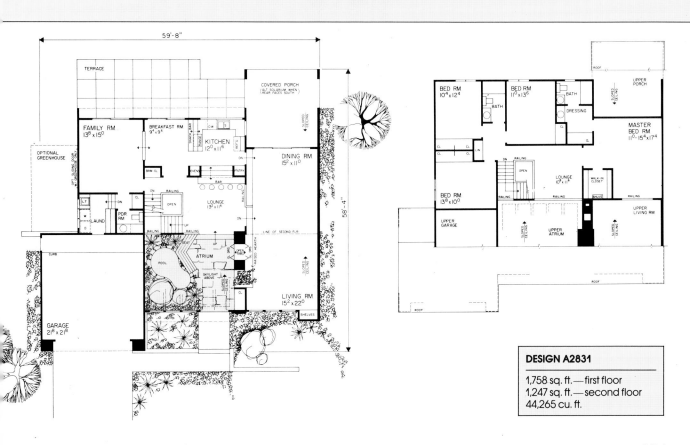

DESIGN A2831

1,758 sq. ft.—first floor
1,247 sq. ft.—second floor
44,265 cu. ft.

ATRIUMS 4

Passive solar heating is a significant highlight of this contemporary home. The huge skylight over the center atrium provides shelter during inclement weather, while admitting plenty of natural light to the atrium and the surrounding rooms. The stone floor will absorb heat from the sun during the day and permit circulation of warm air to other areas at night. During the summer, retractable shades afford protection from the sun without sacrificing the light and the feeling of spaciousness the atrium provides. Sloping ceilings highlight each of the major rooms: three bedrooms, the formal living and dining rooms, and the study. The broad expanses of roof can accommodate solar panels should an active system be desired to supplement the passive features of this design.

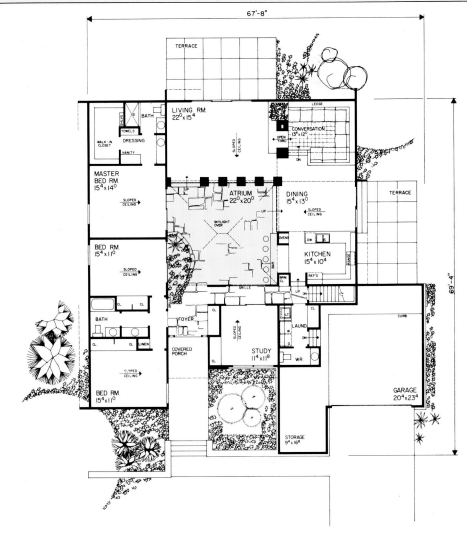

DESIGN A2832

2,805 sq. ft.—excluding atrium
52,235 cu. ft.

A new dimension in living is represented by this unusual contemporary design. Each of the major zones comprises a separate unit that, along with the garage, clusters around the center atrium. High sloped ceilings and plenty of glass areas assure a feeling of spaciousness. The living room offers privacy, while activities in the family room will function easily with the kitchen. A snack bar opens the kitchen to the atrium. There are two strategically located full baths.

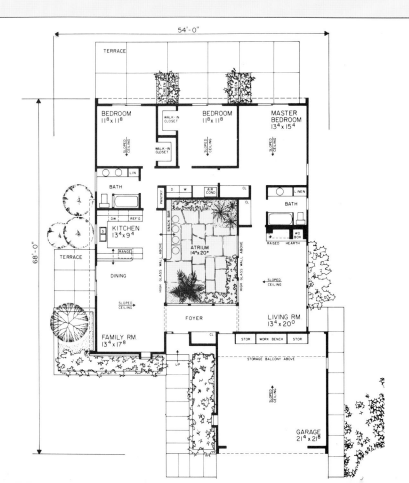

DESIGN A2182

1,558 sq. ft.
280 sq. ft.—atrium
18,606 cu. ft.

PLANS FEATURING ATRIUMS

This versatile contemporary home has much to offer in a relatively small package— three bedrooms, a family room, a mud room, and plenty of storage. The large central atrium is shared by five major rooms, and offers the residents a sense of the outdoors regardless of which room is being used. A spacious terrace helps complete a home plan clearly designed for indoor-outdoor harmony.

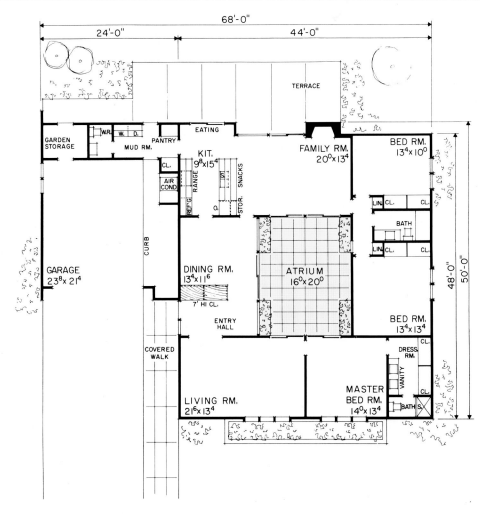

DESIGN A1841

1,920 sq. ft.—excluding atrium
19,806 cu. ft.

The uniqueness of this contemporary house is highlighted by the central atrium. All of the major rooms have visual access to this beautiful space, open to the sky and yet protected by the walls of the house. The varied roof planes contrast dramatically with the simplicity of the vertical siding. Inside there is a feeling of spaciousness resulting from the sloping ceilings. The sleeping zone has four bedrooms, two baths, and plenty of closets.

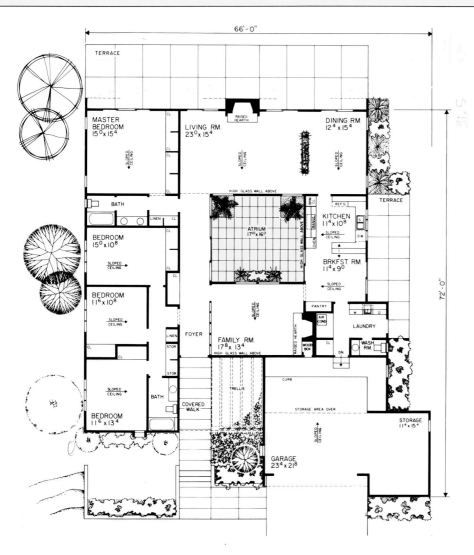

OPTIONAL PARTIAL BASEMENT

DESIGN A2135

2,495 sq. ft.—excluding atrium
28,928 cu. ft.

SUNSPACES

DESCENDED FROM the old-fashioned summertime garden room, sunspaces today are used year-round—indoor spaces with an outdoor ambience designed to reap the sun's warmth and light.

A living space with a sunny disposition is bound to warm the heart, especially on a chilly winter's day. Sunspaces do just that because these glass-enclosed areas take advantage of the sun and lend themselves to multiple uses.

Because they offer the best of two worlds—a visual and aesthetic connection to the outdoors amid the comforts and protection of the indoor environment—sunspaces are a popular feature of many house plans, either as an integral part of the design or as a manufactured unit purchased separately and installed during construction. In addition, manufactured units can be added to an existing structure, often with minimal remodeling.

No more chilly walks to an outdoor spa—soak and take in the view in the warmth and comfort of a sun room.

Manufactured or custom-designed, sunspaces come in a variety of sizes and shapes to suit the configuration of the house. They may be situated upstairs or down, enclosing a balcony or a portion of a deck, spanning the length of the house, projecting into a side yard, or tucked between two wings. They often adjoin heavily used living areas—the living room, kitchen, or family room. And although the sunspace is descended from the old-fashioned garden room and Victorian-era solarium—a summertime sitting room filled with porch furniture and plenty of plants—modern versions are well insulated, and most can double for almost any activity all year long.

Sunspaces should be positioned to receive as much sunlight as possible during the winter months, preferably along a southern exposure. Of course, the shape of your lot and preferred views may dictate the possible orientations. But a north-facing sunspace, or one that receives no direct sunlight, makes a cool and gloomy living space.

Basically there are two types of sunspaces—greenhouses and solariums—each with as many variations as there are house plans. *Greenhouses* are meant mostly for the cultivation of plants, and sometimes to collect and store heat from the sun to help warm the rest of the house. *Solariums* are intended as living spaces, positioned to take advantage of views as well as plentiful natural light, and furnished to function as an indoor room. These are not strict categories, though, and many sunspaces serve more than one purpose: a greenhouse that's well ventilated and climate-controlled invites people as well as plants to enjoy the indoor-outdoor atmosphere; and a well-insulated, south-facing solarium with a thick masonry floor may work as a partial solar collector even though it was not designed for that function.

A greenhouse is a glazed structure intended primarily for gardening. It may be free-standing—glass-enclosed on all four sides—or attached to a wall of the house. Because it is meant for cultivating plants, a greenhouse is often single-glazed—each panel formed by a single pane of double-strength glass—and may not be fully weathertight. Since circulating air and moisture are a must for plants, most greenhouses have an adjustable roof sash at the ridge, and often come equipped with a fan and wall ventilators.

A *solar greenhouse* is a sunspace designed specifically to save energy by producing a portion of the heat intended for household use. Because it functions as a passive collector of solar heat, this type of greenhouse is usually constructed as an integral part of the house and requires, among other things, floor and wall surfaces and a ventilation system all engineered to trap and store the sun's heat and distribute the warmth to the interior rooms. A solar greenhouse demands a southern exposure, and works most efficiently when tightly insulated from the foundation up and equipped with double- or triple-glazing. To offset the discomforts of too much summer heat, or long stretches of winter overcast with little sun, the solar greenhouse can be closed off from the interior by sliding glass doors and/or windows.

Another type of sunspace is the *garden room/sun room*, an area adjacent to the home's regular living spaces but separated from them by glass doors and/or windows. Examples of this are a spa enclosure, an eating area near the kitchen, or perhaps a room for plants located off the living room. When the doors are open, these sunspaces become extensions of the rooms they adjoin; when closed off, they offer a visual connection to the outdoors. Like greenhouses, these rooms require adequate insulation and a good ventilation system for maximum comfort.

Manufactured greenhouses may be attached to existing houses with little or no modification. A neat fit, this one smoothly extends the roofline of the house.

The *solarium* is perhaps the most versatile of sunspaces. It functions as a principal living space on a year-round basis—a major component of the home, completely or partially open to adjoining rooms and easily accessible from other areas of the house. The solarium is an indoor room with an outdoor ambience, and often replaces the standard living, dining, or family room in a plan. As a room for living, its roof and walls of glass must be fully insulated and the roof area in particular equipped with shades or blinds to protect carpets and furnishings from fading and de-terioration caused by the sun. Solariums, like other rooms, are more en-joyable when built with windows or doors to vent extra heat and admit fresh breezes. And, though plants and people may do well together in the solarium, this light-filled space is intended mainly for people to enjoy outdoor living indoors.

SUNSPACES

1 *A wood frame, a wood floor, and the maximum use of glass create a sun room that almost seems part of the forest.*

2, 3 *Using prefabricated greenhouse components, the architect has custom designed a structure that fits snugly between two walls and wraps around a corner of the house. A colorful adjunct to the deck, it is also visible and accessible from within.*

4 *When winter comes and the landscape is bare, flowers will still be blooming in the greenhouse.*

1

2

3

4

1

2

3

4

1 *A greenhouse within a sun room assures that both people and plants will enjoy an optimal environment. The spacious and cheerful sun room can be reached from deck, living room, and dining room; and the door inside it leads to the greenhouse, which shares a window with the study.*

2 *Insulated panels roll down to make this sun room suitable for any season. Prefabricated and added after the house was built, it's perfect for starting seeds in winter and for enjoying the view anytime.*

3 *Light floods this solarium from three sources, including French doors and skylights that open. A partial brick floor makes watering plants worry-free—and is a surprising but harmonious design element. The brick also retains moisture, which gives off humidity that plants love.*

4 *For unparalleled light and a sense of openness, no room in the house compares to a solarium. It gives you the outdoors with all the indoor comforts—truly a blessing on a chilly afternoon.*

SUNSPACES 1

This comfortable traditional home offers plenty in the way of modern livability. For starters, there is the light-filled greenhouse/sun room, accessible from both the large country kitchen and the clutter room and certain to be a focal point of casual entertaining. There is a media room, perfect for stereo listening and video watching. The house also features a formal dining room, a living room with a fireplace, a covered porch, and three bedrooms, including a well-planned master suite.

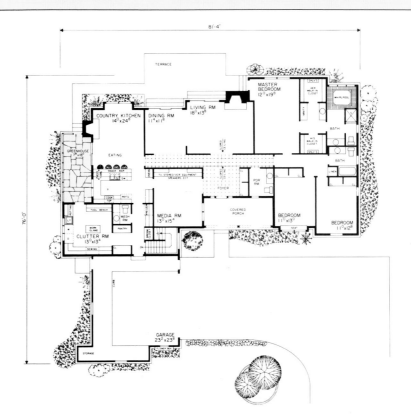

DESIGN A2880

2,758 sq. ft.—living area
149 sq. ft.—greenhouse
60,850 cu. ft.

SUNSPACES 2

Passive solar techniques and an active solar component work together to help heat and cool this striking contemporary home. The lower-level solarium is the primary passive element—in addition to being an attractive room in its own right, complete with a whirlpool spa. It admits sunlight during the day for direct-gain heating. The warmth, absorbed into the thermal floor, is then radiated into the structure at night. The earth berms on three sides of the lower level help keep out winter cold and summer heat.

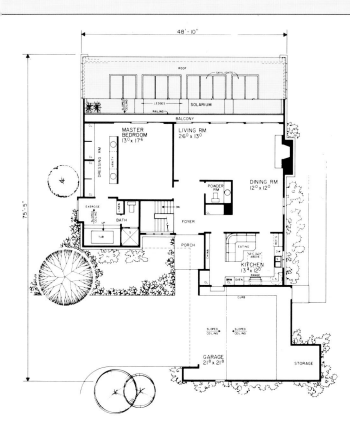

DESIGN A2835

1,626 sq. ft.—main level
2,038 sq. ft.—lower level
50,926 cu. ft.

SUNSPACES 3

This compact design has pleasing wide overhangs, a privacy wall in front, and vertical windows. Sure to please everyone is the 216-square-foot sunspace with view windows for sunning or leisurely breakfasts. The courtyard created by the front privacy wall further enhances the outstanding indoor-outdoor living possibilities of this contemporary home. Open planning combines a sloped-ceiling living room with a rear dining room that opens to the sunspace and functional kitchen nearby. The three bedrooms include a master suite with its own whirlpool spa.

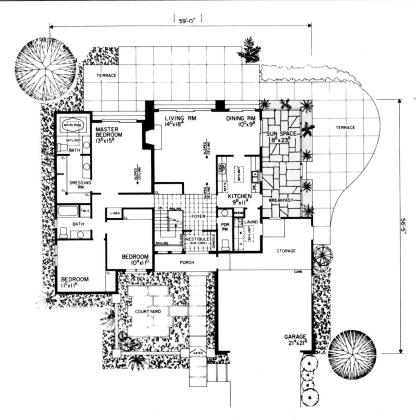

DESIGN A2902

1,632 sq. ft.
40,723 cu. ft.

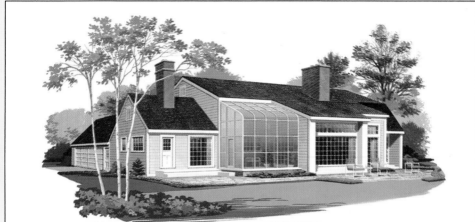

SUNSPACES 4

The traditional styling of the streetside facade of this house offers no hint of the dramatic, light-filled rear elevation. Not only is there an attractive greenhouse/sun room (which can double as a dining room) with access to both gathering room and kitchen, there are also floor-to-ceiling windows and sliding glass doors that provide easy and immediate use of the terraces during warm weather. The master bedroom suite is privately contained on the first floor, as is a quiet study off the foyer. Note the convenient mudroom and laundry with access from both kitchen and garage. Three more bedrooms and a lounge are located on the second floor.

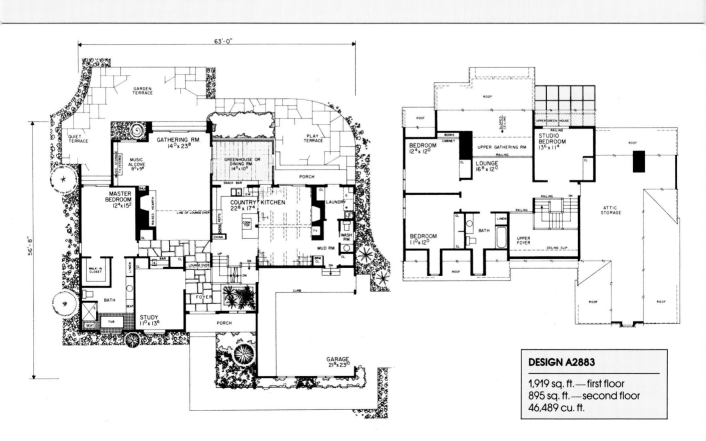

DESIGN A2883

1,919 sq. ft.—first floor
895 sq. ft.—second floor
46,489 cu. ft.

PLANS FEATURING SUNSPACES

SUNSPACES 5

This traditionally-styled house features bay windows, shutters, a fanlight and a cupola on the roof. A sun room is in the rear corner of the house, adjacent to the kitchen. Its sloped ceiling and glass walls open this room to the outdoors. Also adjacent to the kitchen is a "clutter room"—it includes a workshop, laundry, pantry, and washroom.

DESIGN A2921

3,215 sq. ft.—first floor
296 sq. ft.—sun room
711 sq. ft.—second floor
69,991 cu. ft.

SUNSPACES 6

This is a contemporary design, both inside and out. Inside are two sunspaces that will help heat the house in winter using the principles of passive solar collection. The larger sunspace is accessible from the formal living room, the dining room, and the gathering room, making it a likely area to handle an over-flow crowd for large-scale entertaining. The second sun-space, right off the master bath, is completely private and features a hot tub. The central enclosed entry acts as both a foyer and a gallery. With clerestory windows above, this is a space that will always be light and cheerful even though it is in the center of the house. Check the rest of the plan carefully to see how well it has been thought out for successful family living.

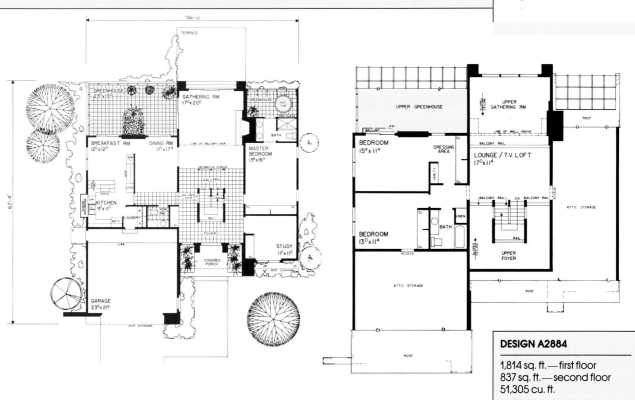

DESIGN A2884

1,814 sq. ft. — first floor
837 sq. ft. — second floor
51,305 cu. ft.

PLANS FEATURING SUNSPACES

SUNSPACES 7

This passive solar home offers 4,200 square feet of living space on three different levels. The primary passive element is the lower-level sun room, which admits sunlight for direct-gain heating. The solar warmth collected in the sun room will radiate into the rest of the house after it passes through the sliding glass doors. During the warm summer months, shades are put over the skylight to protect it from direct sunlight and excessive heat build-up. This design also has the option of incorporating active solar panels to the roof, which would be installed on the south-facing portion of the roof.

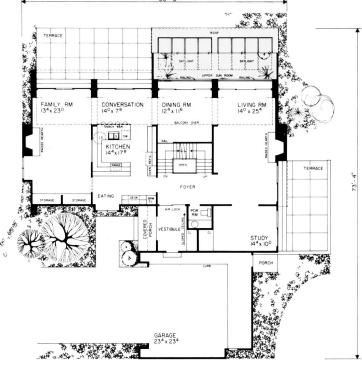

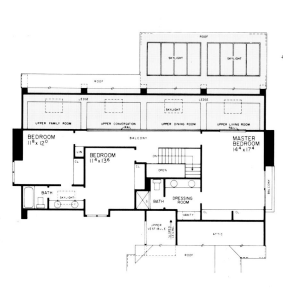

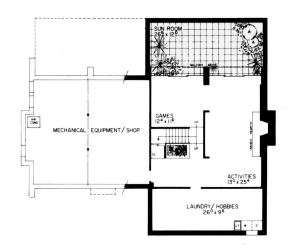

DESIGN A2834

1,775 sq. ft.—main level
1,041 sq. ft.—upper level
1,128 sq. ft.—lower level
55,690 cu. ft.

SUNSPACES 8

The solarium in this traditional home is located where three rooms—the master bedroom, the living room, and the dining room—can take full advantage of its aesthetic appeal. All three rooms have sliding glass doors that lead to the solarium, making it easy to use as an auxiliary space during large parties, or as a relaxing retreat from the bedroom. Note also the private outside entrance to the master bedroom, with its own flower court visible from the living room. Two terraces to the rear add to the possibilities for outdoor living, one off the family room, the other off the solarium and master bedroom.

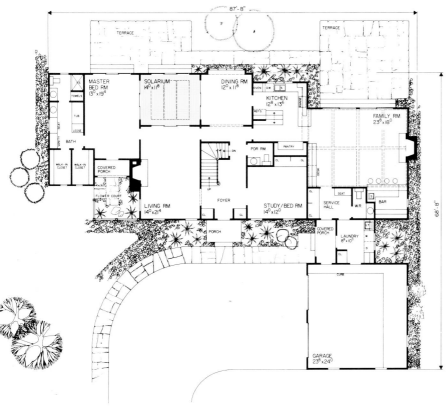

DESIGN A2615

2,563 sq. ft.—first floor
552 sq. ft.—second floor
59,513 cu. ft.

PLANS FEATURING SUNSPACES

SUNSPACES 9

This energy-efficient home features passive solar collection via the solarium and the earth berms. The berms help keep the house cool in the summer and insulate against heat loss in the winter. In addition, the south-facing roof of the dining room, gathering room, and study is almost all glass for plenty of light and warmth. The solarium, open at two levels, brings a bit of the outdoors to the inside rooms, in combination with a sunken outdoor garden, from which it is separated by a glass wall. This unusual design innovation will add a special quality to the entire house.

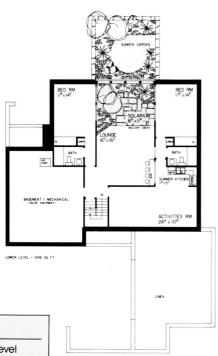

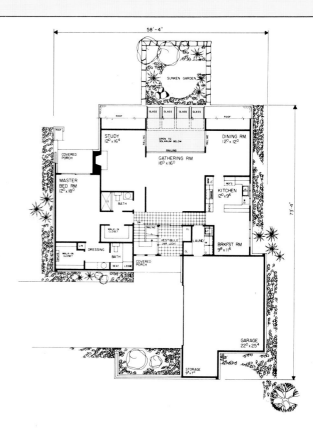

DESIGN A2830

1,795 sq. ft.—main level
1,546 sq. ft.—lower level
49,900 cu. ft.

SUNSPACES 10

Here is an energy-efficient design that makes the most of an open plan. The walls and ceiling of the corner garden room are made of glass, so that the room can be seen and enjoyed from the living and dining area, as well as from the family room. The garden room will act as a passive solar collector, giving off gentle warmth in the winter months. The earth berms on either side of the house will provide excellent insulation. Note that the walled entrance court would act as a sun trap even in the cool days of fall and winter. The entire back of the house opens onto the large terrace, making it perfect for warm-weather living and entertaining.

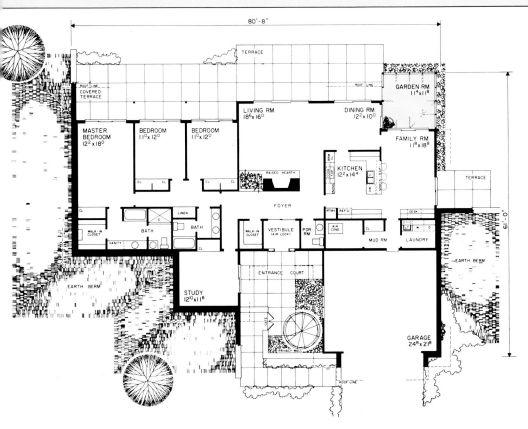

DESIGN A2903

2,555 sq. ft.
32,044 cu. ft.

SUNSPACES 11

Bay windows highlight the front and side exteriors of this three-bedroom Colonial-style home. For energy efficiency, this design has a 576-square-foot solar garden room, destined to be one of the most popular gathering spots in the house. This passive solar collector opens onto the family room, breakfast room, and second-floor master suite, effectively increasing the visual space of each. In addition to helping with winter heating, this garden room will offer pleasant views of the adjoining terrace and the garden beyond.

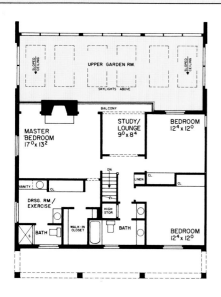

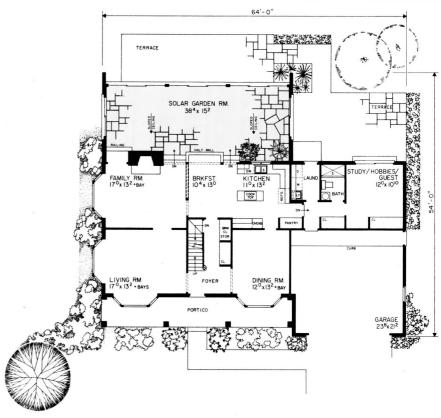

DESIGN A2839

2,141 sq. ft. — first floor
1,120 sq. ft. — second floor
58,925 cu. ft.

144

SUNSPACES 12

Earth berms shelter the interior of this house from both the cold of winter and the heat of summer. The south-facing sun room—a light-filled area with a stone floor to absorb heat—provides passive solar capability (not to mention a pleasant living space). When needed, the heat will be circulated to the interior by opening the sliding glass doors or by mechanical means. A large, centrally located skylight creates an open feeling and lights up the interior, where the formal and informal living areas are located. The sun room contains 425 square feet of space.

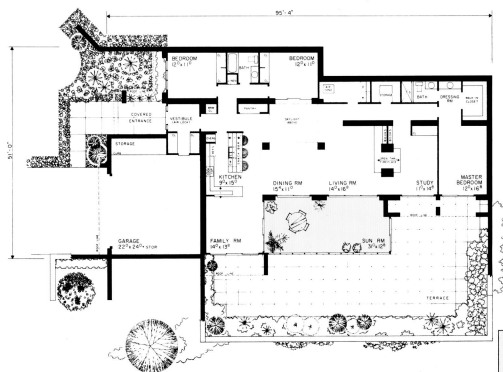

DESIGN A2862

2,808 sq. ft.
37,219 cu. ft.

SUNSPACES 13

This luxurious three-bed-
room house offers comfort
on many levels. The unusual
design incorporates a rear
garden room connected to a
conversation pit off the living
room. The combination of
fireplace, conversation pit,
and garden room is sure to
be extremely attractive to
both family and friends. The
adjacent family room has a
high sloped ceiling, complete
with skylights. Other features
include an entrance court,
an activities room, a modern
kitchen, an upper-level
lounge, and a master bed-
room with its own balcony.

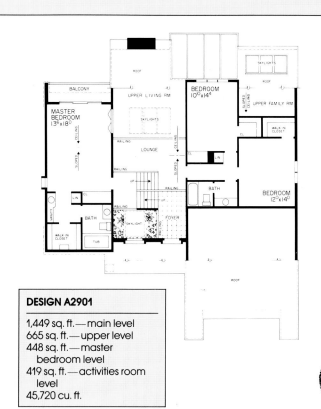

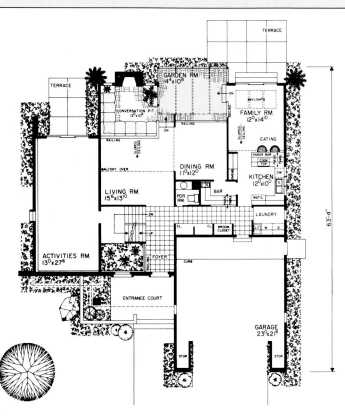

DESIGN A2901

1,449 sq. ft.—main level
665 sq. ft.—upper level
448 sq. ft.—master
   bedroom level
419 sq. ft.—activities room
   level
45,720 cu. ft.

146

SUNSPACES 14

The entrance steps lead through a low-walled entrance court to the front door and a glass-roofed garden room—a plan built around indoor-outdoor living. There are two terraces, one on either side of the house, accessible from numerous sliding glass doors. The large number of windows and glass doors featured in this design will make the house light-filled and cheery from one season to the next. Take note of the through-fireplace that separates the living and dining rooms, while allowing both to enjoy the same fire.

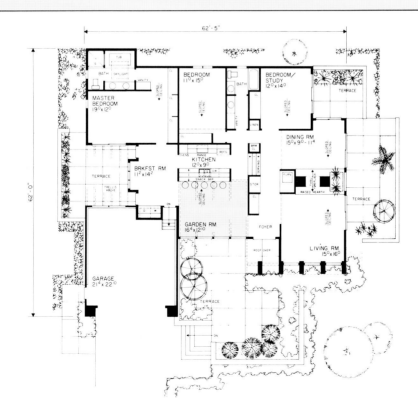

DESIGN A2858

2,231 sq. ft.
28,150 cu. ft.

An attractive, traditionally styled family house, this plan also features a sunny greenhouse space off the country kitchen. This convenient location assures that the plants in the greenhouse will be taken care of regularly and also allows all members of the family to enjoy the indoor garden on a daily basis. Note the two fireplaces—one in the country kitchen and one in the formal living room. The first floor also contains a practical hobby room in between the garage and the kitchen—right where it belongs—and a study in a quiet location off the foyer. Four bedrooms and two full baths are on the second floor.

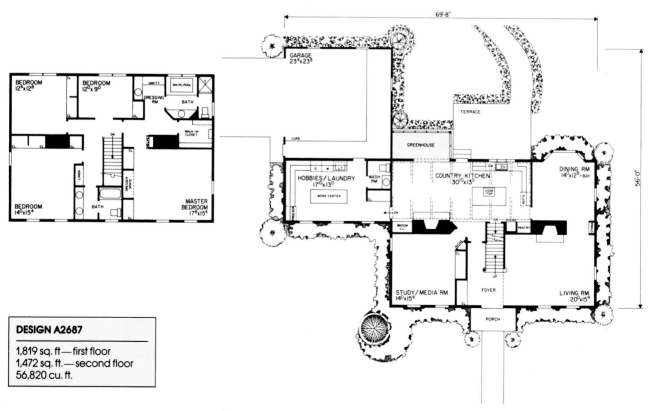

DESIGN A2687

1,819 sq. ft—first floor
1,472 sq. ft.—second floor
56,820 cu. ft.

If you are looking for an informal, open plan that doesn't sacrifice privacy or interest, look carefully at this design. There is a combination dining and living room with a fireplace, a separate media room, a very private and complete master suite (including a whirlpool spa), and an appealing combination of country kitchen, clutter room, and greenhouse. These three rooms work together well to satisfy the practical needs of a family and to provide an unusually attractive living area. The greenhouse is accessible from both the country kitchen and the clutter room, making it an ideal place to putter about, tending plants or relaxing, whenever you have a few moments to spare from the activities of the day.

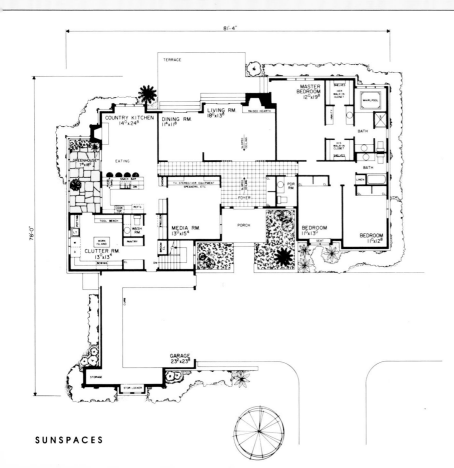

DESIGN A2915

2,758 sq. ft.
60,850 cu. ft.

SUNSPACES 17

A combination of textures—stone, wood, and glass—on the exterior of this contemporary house gives it special appeal. There is a delightful greenhouse accessible from both the living room and dining room, to use for plants and as an enjoyable spot to lounge. Note how indoor-outdoor living is highlighted with the bay window in the kitchen, the front terrace with its exposed beams, and the large window in the living room, which offers an unimpeded view of the rear terrace and garden. All three bedrooms are zoned carefully to one side of the central foyer to allow privacy and quiet.

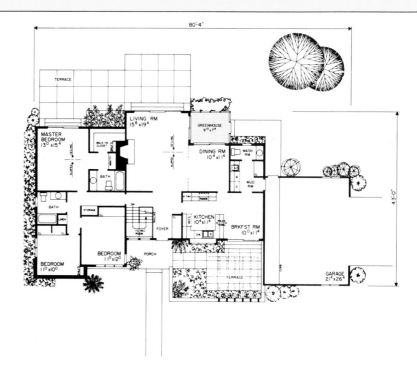

DESIGN A2871

1,824 sq. ft.
44,590 cu. ft.

SUNSPACES 18

Take a careful look at the plan for this contemporary home. Note how the lower level contains two bedrooms, a utility room, an activities room and an adjacent conversation lounge with a fireplace, and a sunny solarium open to the upper floor. Skylights and tall windows will help this space act as a passive solar collector. Entrance is on the upper level, through a private garden court. The master bedroom and quiet study area are on the upper level, as are the kitchen, living room, and dining room. For outdoor living, there is a large deck accessible from the dining room and kitchen, an ideal location for warm-weather dining.

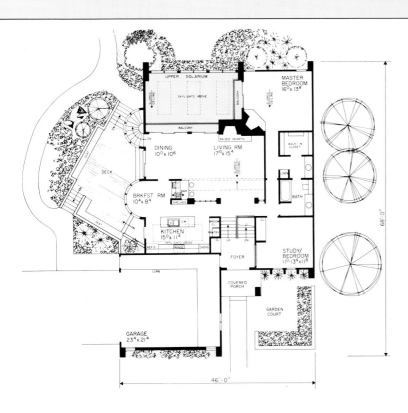

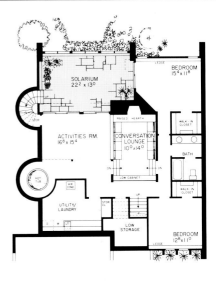

DESIGN A2827

1,618 sq. ft. — upper level
1,458 sq. ft. — lower level
41,370 cu. ft.

POOLS & SPAS

AS AN AT-HOME RECREATION CENTER for the whole family, the swimming pool ranks high on the list, but its smaller relation, the spa, is making waves too as a warm-water retreat for outdoor relaxation.

A swimming pool or spa adds a refreshing dimension to outdoor living and informal entertaining—from leisurely sunbathing to a noisy, splashing game of water tag. Although swimming pools represent a major investment in dollars, they provide a substantial return in terms of pleasure as an at-home recreation center for the whole family. Increased health awareness has made physical fitness a high priority for many people, and swimming pools offer invigorating exercise for all ages. Spas, too, offer health benefits for therapeutic bathing and after-work relaxation.

In addition to the pleasure it provides as an outdoor living space, a swimming pool or spa and its immediate surroundings enhance the appearance of the house and garden. Because of its size, a swimming pool is usually the dominant feature of a landscape, and attention must be given to its placement on the site—especially its relationship to the house and overall proportion, design, and materials.

Some house plans, like those in this chapter, include a pool design, already sized and styled to suit the building's architecture. Many homeowners, however, prefer to situate the pool farther from the house, for better exposure to the sun, or to set it apart as a separate entertaining area. There are several points to consider in making the decision about pool size, shape, and placement.

One of the first questions to ask is, "Who will use the pool, and how?" A family pool to be enjoyed by both children and adults should have a large shallow area at one end and possibly even a little wading pool to one side. If there are several children in the family, the pool needs to be big enough to allow swimming and play activities simultaneously. A pool intended mostly for exercise, or for the athlete in training, has different

With wood decking and stone accents, this spa is creatively integrated into an oriental-style landscape.

requirements. A pool for swimming laps is long, relatively narrow, and deep enough to permit easy turnarounds. A pool for diving is usually deep at both ends, with its shallow area in the middle.

Another consideration is where to put the pool. A large, flat lot with few mature trees offers more flexibility for siting than a long, narrow lot or one that climbs a hillside. Exposure to sun and wind is an important factor for comfort. In most parts of the country a southern exposure offers the greatest amount of sun, but a western orientation works well too. Light breezes can make poolside sitting more comfortable on a hot afternoon, but too much wind on a cooler day can drive swimmers indoors. Both sun and wind can be moderated with strategically placed screens of one sort or another—trees (beware of varieties that might shed their leaves into the pool), fences, or hedges.

Shapes and styles of swimming pools today are tremendously varied. In past years, traditional and period house styles—New England Colonial, Tudor, or French Provincial, for example—were nearly always associated with formal pool shapes, such as the oval or rectangle. Contemporary-style houses invariably displayed kidney-shaped pools. Today there is much more flexibility in pool design and a growing interest in naturalistic pool settings to complement any style house. The natural approach employs shapes that echo the contours of the site, using smooth rocks for the pool surround and boulders for sitting, and coordinating poolside plantings with the natural landscape.

Most swimming pools of the 1980s are one of three types: constructed of gunite, an air-sprayed concrete that is extremely strong; vinyl-lined (actually a huge vinyl container supported by a sturdy wall system); or fiberglass. Gunite pools are the most versatile because the concrete will adhere to any excavated shape, and its plaster finish can be tinted any color desired. Gunite pools can also be painted or tiled, though the latter finish is expensive. Vinyl-lined and fiberglass pools are manufactured in several colors, the tint built into the material at the factory. Because the color of the pool influences the apparent shade of the water, it's wise to consider the finish, the pool deck, and adjacent landscaping all at the same time.

Pool decks function like patios in many ways—as places to sit and sun, entertain guests, or set up table and chairs for dining—and often are constructed of the same materials as patios. Concrete, brick, granite, fieldstone, or tile, used individually or in combination, are all excellent materials to set off the pool. Concrete is a favorite material for pool surrounds because of its reasonable cost, ease of installation, and perma-

For privacy and all-weather use, consider locating your spa in a sun room.

nence. Its roughened surface is basically slip-free, unlike some other forms of masonry. A wooden deck, well sanded against splinters and sealed to prevent water damage, is a good solution for a pool built on uneven terrain.

Whatever material you choose for poolside paving, it's important to make the area large enough to accommodate comfortable furnishings and provide plenty of elbow room. As a rule of thumb, the area for poolside activities should be at least equal to the area of the pool itself. If there's enough room, a poolhouse with changing rooms, a bathroom, an eating/entertainment area, an outdoor shower, a sauna, and a comfortable place to sit in the shade add up to the ultimate in poolside living. If a poolhouse or cabaña is not in your budget now, consider a simple awning outside the doors most often used to get to the pool. Such a shaded spot, furnished with a few chairs and a table, will add greatly to your enjoyment of the pool.

Because a spa is small in scale and does not dominate the landscape, it can be situated in any number of places close to the house, or even in a courtyard or sunspace. Many homeowners like to put the spa just off the master bedroom to make it easily accessible for evening or early-morning soaks, and to minimize travel in the cool outside air. If the spa is intended for family use, or for soaking with guests, it's better to place it in a more central location, perhaps near the family room.

Like swimming pools, spas can be vinyl-lined or constructed of gunite or fiberglass. Gunite spas are most often built as an integral part of an in-ground swimming pool design. Separately built spas, however, are typically fabricated of fiberglass or acrylic and sold as a complete unit ready to be installed in the ground. A cousin to the spa, the wooden hot tub also serves as a relaxing warm-water retreat, but it is designed for above-ground installation and requires proper structural support.

Boulders in the landscape and a freeform swimming pool make fieldstone a perfect choice for a poolside surface.

1

1 When a pool is carefully designed to harmonize with its surroundings, the effect can be stunning Here the curves of the pool and steps echo the arch above the terrace, and the color of the stone surround matches the blue of the roof. The result is a formal pool area that complements the symmetrical elegance of the house.

2 A seat in the shade is essential for complete poolside pleasure.

2

3

3 *Adjacent to the pool, the spa is nestled among flowers like a blue jewel.*

4 *A swimming pool adds a special zest to outdoor entertaining, especially when there is plenty of space for comfortable lounging. This gracefully contoured pool, complete with waterfall, has a generous poolside area and is just three steps away from the terrace.*

4

PLANS FEATURING POOLS & SPAS

POOLS & SPAS 1

With the simple shelter fence across one side of the backyard, the pool and patio area of this contemporary house is enclosed on three sides, offering maximum privacy and wind protection. Study the plan and you will find that it offers a lot of livability. Note the good-sized living room and equally large family room. These spacious rooms are perfect for entertaining. The kitchen is conveniently located to provide easy access to the dining and eating area. Two bedrooms, a full bath, and a master bedroom are in the sleeping area.

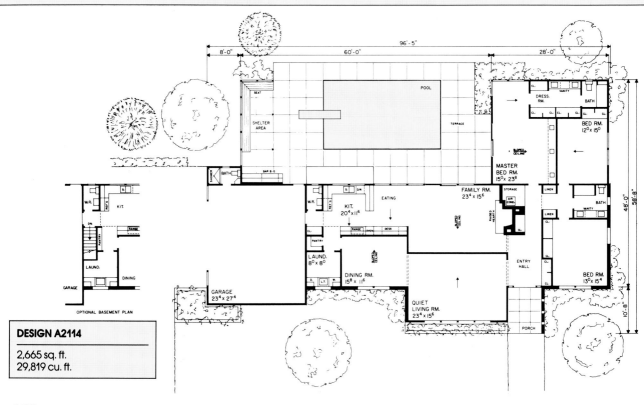

DESIGN A2114

2,665 sq. ft.
29,819 cu. ft.

POOLS & SPAS 2

Picture this gracefully proportioned home sitting on your property. The curving front drive is impressive as it passes the walks to the front door and the service entrance. The spacious family room, kitchen, and breakfast room all face the large patio and pool area. Note the adjacent poolhouse for easy outdoor entertaining. The roof masses, the centered masonry chimney, the window symmetry, and the 108-foot front facade make this a distinctive home. The front room and the family room are of equal size and each has its own fireplace.

DESIGN A1787

2,656 sq. ft.—first floor
744 sq. ft.—second floor
51,164 cu. ft.

POOLS & SPAS 3

This contemporary one-story home should be oriented on a west-facing site, especially if it is built in the northern regions of the country. The plan reflects interesting living patterns and excellent indoor-outdoor relationships. Note how the south-facing side of the house contains numerous sliding glass doors for easy access to the walled patio, pool, and garden area. The north side, on the other hand, has only one small window and will be protected by the privacy wall. Wide overhanging roofs, skylights, glass gables, vented walkways, and wind-buffering privacy fences are among this design's energy-oriented features.

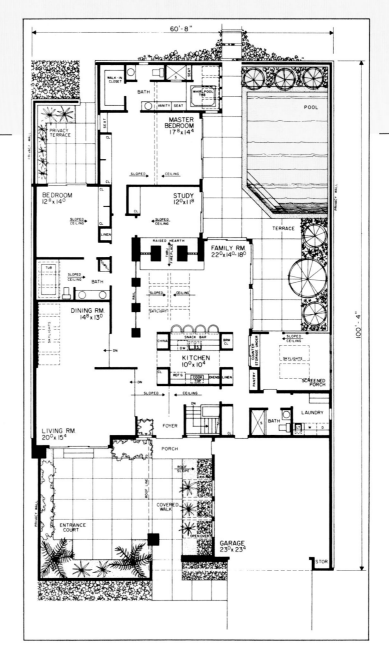

DESIGN A2882

2,832 sq. ft.
59,635 cu. ft.

If yours is a growing, active family, the chances are that family members will want their new home to relate to the outdoors as much as possible. This distinctive design puts a premium on private outdoor living. You don't even have to install the proposed swimming pool to get the most enjoyment from this home. Developing this area as an enclosed garden court would also open the indoor living areas to the natural beauty of the outdoors. Notice the fine zoning of the plan and how each area has sliding glass doors to provide an unrestricted outdoor view. Three bedrooms and a study are serviced by three baths. The family and gathering rooms provide two great living areas.

95'-8"

TERRACE

BED. RM.
17⁴×12⁰

STUDY
11⁰ × 11⁰

MASTER
BED. RM.
13⁰ × 17⁴

BATH

WALK-IN
CL.

BATH

LINEN

DRESS.
RM.

GATE

BED. RM.
13⁴×10⁰

BATH

CL.

FAMILY RM.
13⁴×19⁴

TERRACE

TERRACE

POOL

RAISED HEARTH

74'-4"

CURB

PDR.
RM.

SNACKS

OVENS

PANTRY

CL.

KIT.
11⁰ × 13⁰

RANGE

LNDRY.

NOOK
9⁸ × 13⁰

DINING RM.
12⁰ × 17⁴

FOYER

RAISED HEARTH

PORCH

GARAGE
22⁸ × 25⁰

GATHERING RM.
17⁴ × 26⁸

DESIGN A2343

3,110 sq. ft.
51,758 cu. ft.

POOLS & SPAS 5

With five bedrooms, plus a library, a game room, an activities room, and a hobby room, the active family will have an abundance of indoor space to enjoy individual pursuits. And look at the outdoor space: a huge patio and pool area is located toward the rear of the house for optimal privacy. The long balcony provides direct outdoor access from all the rooms on the upper floor. A study of both levels reveals that the major living areas look out on the patio-pool area, with perhaps a pleasant view beyond that. Even the kitchen, with its large window over the sink, has a view.

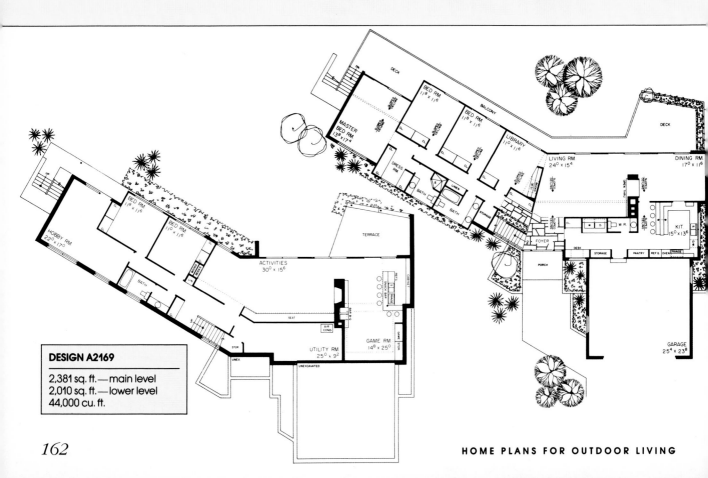

DESIGN A2169

2,381 sq. ft.—main level
2,010 sq. ft.—lower level
44,000 cu. ft.

POOLS & SPAS 6

The irregular shape of this sprawling ranch-style home is enhanced by the low-pitched, wide overhanging roof. From the main living area of the house two wings project to help form an appealing semi-private entrance court. Variations in grade result in a lower-level garage. The patio and proposed pool area are easily reached through the family room and the bedroom wing, and are the most likely spots for the younger members of the family to congregate. The master bedroom is nicely isolated from the rest of the house.

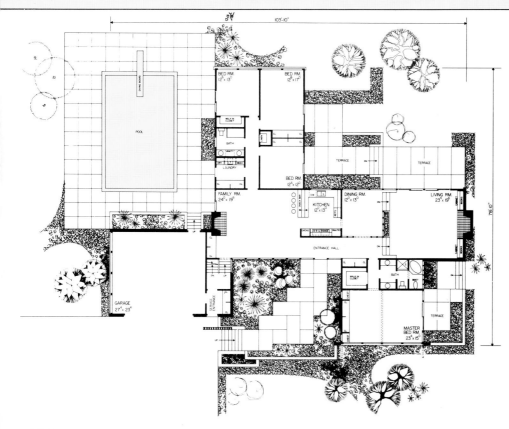

DESIGN A2251

3,112 sq. ft.
36,453 cu. ft.

The wide-open atmosphere of the Southwest is captured in this extraordinary Spanish-style home. Its features are legion, both inside and out. There are four separate outdoor terraces, a covered porch, and a good-sized swimming pool. Note how the pool is sited next to the family room and kitchen for convenience and eye appeal. The interior is divided into three main areas: the sleeping wing, the formal living and dining zone, and the informal family room–kitchen area. Notice how easily each of these areas functions with the outdoors.

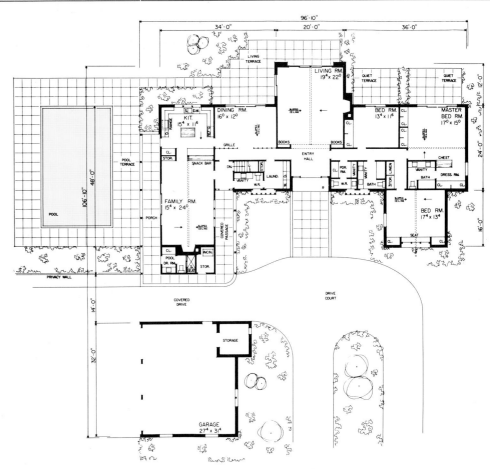

DESIGN A1725

3,242 sq. ft.
44,316 cu. ft.

164

This is a unique contemporary adaptation of a ranch-style home. Special attention has been paid to outdoor living with the special cook porch off the family room, leading directly to the swimming pool and dining terrace. It doesn't take a lot of imagination to see how much use this area would receive during warm weather. The bedroom wing is well away from the pool area, a thoughtful design consideration. Note how both the breakfast room and the kitchen look out to an enclosed flower court—a delightful view while cooking and dining. Plenty of floor-to-ceiling windows will bring the outdoors in, even in the cool months of the year.

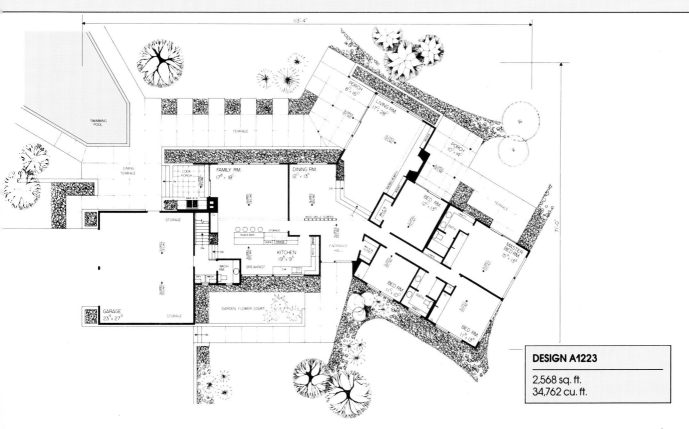

DESIGN A1223

2,568 sq. ft.
34,762 cu. ft.

PUTTING IT ALL TOGETHER

SOME HOMEOWNERS favor house plans that provide multiple opportunities for outdoor living in a single design and enjoy the challenge of integrating landscape, furnishings, and accessories.

Sometimes a roomy brick patio, or a pair of balconies, or even a big wraparound porch doesn't offer enough in the way of outdoor living. Perhaps the view from the site is so spectacular that it calls for a network of sitting and dining areas, upstairs and down; or the property may be so large that the terrace can extend out to surround a swimming pool and join a gazebo and flower garden. Perhaps, on the other hand, the lot is modest in size and flanked by nearby houses. A plan that looks mostly inward for its outdoor living spaces might be just the answer, incorporating a small plant-screened patio and featuring a large, completely private atrium or courtyard living space at the heart of the design.

For many homeowners, a plan that provides multiple opportunities for outdoor living close at hand offers the best of several worlds. The house plans in this chapter combine a number of possibilities in a single configuration, and have been designed to permit the different indoor-outdoor elements to function smoothly together visually and physically. Some plans are traditional in style, and some are contemporary, but all emphasize different arrangements for the enjoyment of indoor-outdoor living. Generally speaking, this collection of plans is more complex than those presented in previous chapters—not more difficult to understand, or more complicated to build from the contractor's point of view, but more challenging for the homeowner to "put together" in terms of landscaping, furnishings, and outdoor accents.

Good planning makes all the difference. This modest yard makes thorough use of its space—with a deck, pool, spa, and garden.

When considering this group of plans, as when shopping for any home plan, it's wise to make a list of family wants and needs to help decide which combination of outdoor spaces is most suitable. It also helps to map out how the spaces will be used. Which areas will work best for entertaining? Where will the children play? What about recreation or gardening? If an outdoor space is meant to serve just one area of the house—like a balcony off the formal dining room—will another area elsewhere handle informal entertaining? This kind of mapping also makes it easier to devise a landscape plan for each area as well as the whole, and to choose the most appropriate materials and accents.

In considering how to unify the various outdoor elements and integrate them with the house and its interior, it's desirable to aim for a balance between adjacent indoor-outdoor spaces in materials, colors, and scale and style of furnishings. Materials don't have to match, but they should make a smooth transition in color and texture from one area to the other. A dark hardwood floor, for example, will meet with a weathered wood deck or a gray slate terrace more gracefully than with a walkway of crushed white rock. A lacy wrought-iron table and chairs probably don't belong on a concrete patio just outside the sliding glass doors of a sleek-lined contemporary, but may be perfectly at home on a brick terrace adjacent to the traditionally furnished living room of a French Provincial design.

Another goal is to aim for balance and harmony between the outdoor living areas of the plan and the overall landscape they adjoin. A two-story house featuring a low-walled courtyard on one side and a large open patio-pool area at the rear demands a certain amount of landscaping coordination. The house will appear less bulky in size and more at ease with its surroundings with a landscape plan that includes groupings of tall trees, flowering shrubs or hedges of medium height, and perhaps a garden structure in another part of the yard to balance the house and act as a focal point.

It can be a real challenge to come up with a design that ties together all of the elements in a landscape smoothly. It's often best to seek the assistance of a professional. One possibility, of course, is to turn over the whole project to a landscape architect or designer. But if you want to be involved with all aspects of planning your home, you might choose simply to get some expert advice. Perhaps just talking to a knowledgeable nursery employee or an experienced gardener is all that's necessary.

Planning for outdoor living requires thinking about practical considerations, like fences, walkways, and places to sit; decorative features, such as fountains, bridges, or garden sculpture; and other important accents, like lighting stairways for safety. The following chapter, "Outdoor Accents," focuses on some of the possibilities for accenting outdoor living spaces in a variety of ways.

One of the most pleasurable aspects of having multiple outdoor living spaces—and the accents to accompany them—is the opportunity to enjoy different outdoor experiences at different times of the day: morning coffee in a sunny east-facing courtyard; a late-afternoon break to watch the sun set from a west-facing balcony; and perhaps dinner in the glass-roof solarium with a clear view of the stars overhead. Parents with young children especially appreciate the flexibility offered by a number of outdoor play spaces—patios for pulling wagons and riding tricycles, grassy lawns for turning somersaults and running through the sprinklers, and porches for all manner of rainy-day recreation. These relatively child-proof outdoor spaces have the added bonus of keeping the noise level down and lessening wear and tear inside the house.

Several of the plans in this section take advantage of a second-story deck or balcony to serve as a roof for a patio or terrace below. This type of double-duty construction provides additional cost savings as well as a pleasant, shaded living space. Such a terrace could be constructed in conjunction with any second-story deck or large balcony, whether it is indicated on the plan or not.

The rewards of outdoor living are too numerous to mention. They encompass the practical benefits of recreation, exercise, and gardening; of visually enlarging adjoining interior rooms; and of providing places for socializing and entertaining. They include the aesthetic rewards of dining al fresco or reading a good book under a shady trellis on a hot afternoon, and the intangible rewards of the scent of flowers, or the sound of a fountain, or a view of distant hills. For all of these reasons and more, home owners and home planners alike are realizing the pleasures of being at home outdoors.

From the sliding glass doors of this contemporary-style house, a sprawling multilevel deck leads out to the pool, providing areas for numerous activities along the way—eating, sunbathing, entertaining, gardening (with both built-in and free-standing planters), and of course swimming. To top it off, a roomy balcony overlooks everything.

1 *A flat and open landscape easily accommodates a large pool, flanked by patio, lawn, and wood decking From the farmhouse porch the view stretches out in four directions. To satisfy the need for wind-protected private outdoor space, the center of the house is devoted to a towering atrium, the beams of which can be seen in the roof. (For an inside look, see page 103.)*

2 *Large and imposing, this traditional house graciously accommodates many outdoor features: a high front porch with an elegantly arched roof, perfect for sheltered people-watching; a porch extension, minus the roof, for full sun; a covered balcony at the side, for more privacy; and last but not least, several small balconies, mostly ornamental.*

This compact contemporary design features many different areas for outdoor living: a half-walled entrance courtyard; a small, partially roofed porch off one of the bedrooms; two separate terraces at the rear of the plan; and a covered porch adjacent to the breakfast room, perfect for outdoor meals during warm weather. Note the snack bar, laundry, and step-saving kitchen. Both the gathering and dining rooms overlook the backyard. Each of the three bedrooms has access to an outdoor area. Two large skylights will brighten the interior.

DESIGN A2892

1,623 sq. ft.—first floor
160 sq. ft.—second floor
38,670 cu. ft.

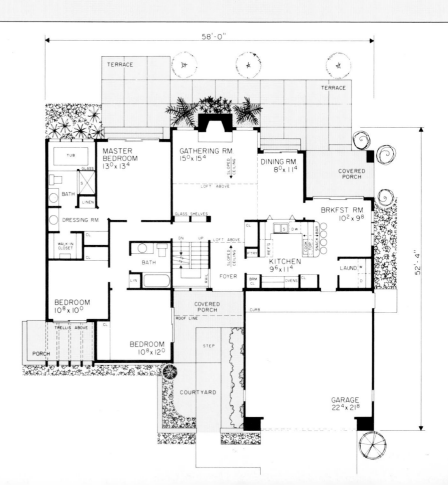

ALL TOGETHER 2

Those who want a traditional home but don't want to sacrifice the pleasures of outdoor living should consider this plan. It is an adaptation of an 18th-century "single house" from Charleston, S.C., so called because it was a single room deep. The house is designed to stand with its narrow end to the street. The plan reveals its commitment to outdoor living with a second-story covered porch and a covered piazza overlooking a walled courtyard complete with a fountain. In addition, there is an open terrace to the side of the house, and a covered porch. Four bedrooms and three full baths are on the second floor; another bedroom and study are on the third floor. The basement has a raised-hearth fireplace, a washroom, and a wine cellar.

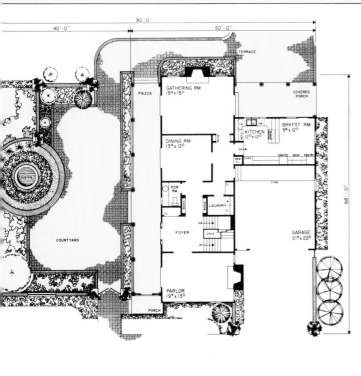

DESIGN A2660

1,479 sq. ft.—first floor
1,501 sq. ft.—second floor
912 sq. ft.—third floor
556 sq. ft.—activities room
 area
57,440 cu. ft.

ALL TOGETHER 3

This charming traditional tri-level home offers loads of comfort for today's lifestyles. The rear deck forms a covered patio on the lower level. The patio-terrace opens to an activities room with its own raised-hearth fireplace, a basement, and an optional bunk room with its own bath. The main level of this stone house includes a convenient kitchen with a snack bar, a dining room, a study, and a large gathering room with a fireplace. That gathering room is continued above with an upper-level gathering room. There's also an upper-level lounge and an upper foyer, in addition to a bedroom and a long bunk room. The large rear deck angles off the kitchen, dining room, and main-level gathering room for plenty of view areas and space for outdoor entertaining.

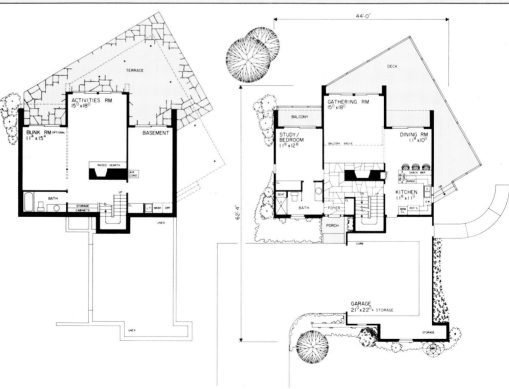

DESIGN A2841

1,044 sq. ft.—main level
851 sq. ft.—upper level
753 sq. ft.—lower level
30,785 cu. ft.

ALL TOGETHER 4

Here is a bold contemporary home where indoor-outdoor living is highlighted. The exciting exteriors show an admirable flair for unusual home design. The varying roof planes and textured blank wall masses protect the streetside facade and give a distinctive appearance. The inclined ramp to the upper main level conjures up the image of a bridge over a moat leading to a castle. Two sets of paneled front doors permit access to either level of the house. The rear exterior projects a veritable battery of balconies, offering direct access to the outdoors for each of the major rooms inside. Note also the two covered outdoor balconies, not to mention a covered terrace.

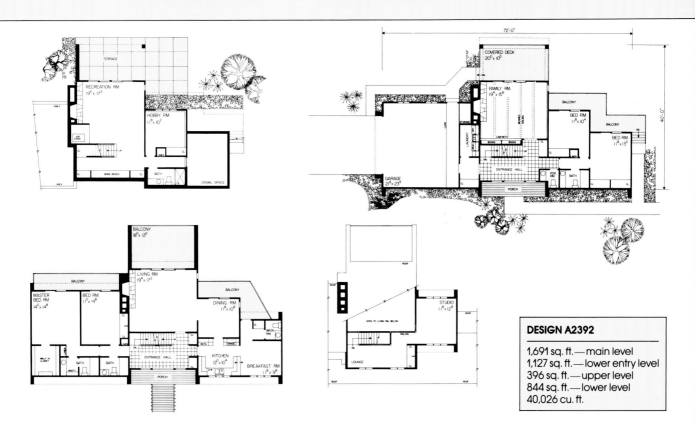

DESIGN A2392

1,691 sq. ft.—main level
1,127 sq. ft.—lower entry level
396 sq. ft.—upper level
844 sq. ft.—lower level
40,026 cu. ft.

OUTDOOR ACCENTS

FROM AWNINGS AND BRIDGES to walks and gazebos, outdoor accents add personality to any home design and can transform an ordinary outdoor area into a unique multipurpose space.

This chapter offers a catalog of features you may want to include in your plans for outdoor living. Fences and gates, walls, walks and steps, trellises and screens, seats and benches, planters, fountains and ponds, hearths, bridges, gazebos, and outdoor lighting don't fall into the category of necessities, but any one of these elements, or a combination of several, can transform an ordinary outdoor area into a personal expression of your interests and taste. Outdoor accents add personality to a design, making your house and garden a unique place in which to live and entertain.

If outdoor living and garden design are new to you, use this chapter as a starting point to develop a list of "must haves." You might also start a scrapbook of pictures cut out of magazines or catalogs and annotated with your own ideas. Visit as many gardens as you can, both public and private, to gather information about what appeals to you. Soon you will have assembled a very personal book of ideas and a clearer image of what you simply must have in your ideal outdoor living area.

While you are still in the planning stages, take a careful look at your house and the surrounding landscape

as a whole, not just the exterior architectural details of the house. For example, if your home is Tudor-style, all the details—deck and porch railings; the type of brickwork used for walls, walks, and steps; the kind of fence and gate; the style of outdoor lighting—should reinforce the Tudor look. In fact, any distinct house style calls for compatible design details to create a harmonious whole. The tasteful combination of appropriate details, indoors and out, is one of the secrets to creating an extraordinary home.

All the outdoor accents discussed in this chapter should be considered in the early planning stages of a landscape design, not tagged on as an afterthought. Even if you are not yet ready for a pond or an outdoor hearth, knowing where you want it to go eventually will help you to integrate it smoothly into the overall design when the time comes. Most of the features presented here can be do-it-yourself projects, so you can incorporate them into your plans on a schedule that meets your time and budget considerations.

FENCES & GATES

The more living you do outdoors, the more necessary it is to ensure your privacy. You might not care to screen your entire yard from the view of your neighbors, but you'll probably want to designate at least one private area for eating, sunbathing, or other leisure activities.

In parts of the country with plenty of land, fences are often viewed negatively as an artificial interruption of the wide-open spaces. But in more congested areas, where every bit of land is at a premium, fences are a desirable landscape feature. If you rarely use your outdoor space, privacy is not much of an issue no matter where you live. But if you plan a house with outdoor living in mind, you will need some kind of fence, wall, hedge, or screen.

A wooden fence is often the easiest solution. Wood may not be as durable as brick or stone, but economy and ease of construction make it the first choice of most homeowners. Styles of wooden fences cover a wide range, from the simplest rough lumber nailed to a post-and-stringer frame to elaborate constructions with decorative posts, latticework, and fine carpentry details. Be careful to match the style of the fence with the style of your house. Even though the fence is not an integral part of the house, it will be perceived as part of the same scene and therefore should contribute to the design as a whole. While you are still in the planning stages, take a look at some of the many books available on fence design and construction. The photographs and plans will suggest ideas for fence styles and offer technical advice on construction.

A fence need not block a view entirely to be effective as a screen. If you find a solid fence too confining, an open-weave construction—such as lattice or louvers—is a good choice. The passing observer will focus on the fence, rather than what is behind it, while the people inside can still enjoy glimpses of the landscape. Vines and plantings will make the fence less conspicuous and further increase privacy.

It is better to build the deck, terrace, or patio before building the fence. Once the main structures are in place, you can determine exactly where you want the fence to go. For a preview of what will be screened, get

two or three sturdy eight-foot poles, some heavy wire or clothesline, a couple of old sheets or tarps, and some clothespins. Drive the poles into the ground where you think the fence should go, string the wire or line across the top, and use the clothespins to attach the material. Now sit on the deck or patio and see if a fence in this position does the trick. Also check out the view from across the street and from every available exterior vantage point. A little experimenting at this stage can save costly mistakes later.

Besides providing privacy, a fence defines the perimeter of your outdoor space. Once the boundaries are defined, the design possibilities can be more clearly seen.

Just as fences contain outdoor space, gates break that containment. They offer both passage and a glimpse of what lies beyond the fence, relieving the feeling of being shut in or cooped up. Gates should be built in conformity with the design of the fence and constructed as sturdily as possible, with heavy-duty hinges and some type of cross-bracing to reduce sagging.

A gate covered with a small arbor or roof makes a strong design statement. Such gates are especially appropriate for Colonial, Tudor, and other period houses. The design of a covered gate should be complementary to the style of the house it adjoins. The roof of the gate should echo the roof of the house, not only structurally (in pitch and overall proportions) but also in materials and textures. An arbor gate covered with flowering vines is a particularly charming way to greet a guest.

PRIVACY WALLS

Walls are more substantial in construction than fences, and they make a more substantial aesthetic statement. And although they are considerably more expensive to construct than are wooden fences, in most cases they represent a lifetime improvement to the property.

Brick, stone, and concrete walls are popular with gardeners because of the support they provide to vines and climbers and the way they modify the harsher elements of the climate. A solid wall is an excellent windbreak, and can both trap and store the warmth from the sun. Most of the great gardens of the world employ extensive walls as a part of their design, creating outdoor rooms full of character and charm.

Because of their permanence and solidity, walls give a roomlike feeling to an outdoor space. A fully or partially enclosed entry courtyard gives the feeling of an indoor room, integral to the house, yet open to the sky and surrounded by the pleasures of the garden. To visually tie together your house and outdoor living space, consider using the same material as the exterior walls of the house. If the house is made of both brick and stucco, you could use either material or a combination—for example, stucco walls with ornamental brick posts.

High walls are called for where complete privacy is desired, such as next to a hot tub or spa, or enclosing a private patio off a bedroom or den. In urban settings, where space is at a premium, a high wall is often used at the front edge of the property, enclosing all the space right down to the sidewalk and allowing just a glimpse of the house, perhaps through a wrought-iron gate. These walled city gardens are almost like entry courtyards, except that they surround the entire front of the property. Without such privacy walls, it is unlikely that anyone would want to spend much time in the front yard. With a high wall, however, the homeowner can create a refuge from urban life, perhaps a little oasis with a profusion of plants and a splashing fountain.

Walls do not have to be full height to be effective. A two- or three-foot wall is an excellent means of defining the perimeter of a patio or terrace, doubling as seating when capped with a wide, smooth surface. Similarly, a low wall may be used to create an entry courtyard, mark the edge of a driveway, or set off a smaller area within a large open space, such as a formal herb or rose garden in the middle of a lawn.

To break up the solidity of a garden wall, small openings or *apertures* can be built in. Basically a window without glass, these openings can be strategically placed to offer enticing views. Many traditional walls sport round openings with ornamental grillwork, which are themselves attractive and intriguing.

Generally, walls of any type are not suitable do-it-yourself projects. Brick is probably the easiest material to handle, but even brickwork becomes tricky when it comes to building walls over two or three feet tall. For the best results, it is advisable to have walls constructed by a professional, preferably at the same time as your house is being built so that construction techniques and materials can be easily coordinated.

WALKS & STEPS

When landscape architects use the word *hardscape* they are referring to fences, patios, decks, terraces, trellises, and any other constructed part of the garden. Walks and steps are included in this category, but their importance is often overlooked. In a well-thought-out landscape, walkways and steps guide people from one area or level to the next, offering them the most advantageous views and directing them to specific sites such as a pool or seating area. In addition, the walks and steps should be an attractive element in their own right, constructed of materials in keeping with the house and garden, and providing safe and sure footing in all types of weather.

With a new house and yard it is sometimes difficult to determine the best places to put walkways. One solution is to allow the passage of a year to reveal the natural pathways people use to get from one spot to another, evidenced by beaten-down grass and dusty dirt trails. With this method you can avoid the expense and disappointment of constructing an elaborate walkway only to find that no one uses it.

Traditional designers feel that walkways close to the house should be paved with such building materials as concrete, brick, flagstones, or cobblestones. Moving away from the house and into the more natural environment of the garden, less formal, nonarchitectural materials, such as bark or gravel, should be used. Any loose material, however, should be edged with stones, brick, or lumber to prevent it from being scattered about.

Walkways can be laid out on either straight or curved lines, the choice dictated by your personal preference and by the terrain. A flat landscape can accommodate either straight or curved walkways; uneven terrain usually demands curved paths, or a series of steps to get from one level to another. In formal gardens, paths are most often laid in straight lines or geometric patterns—circular and oval walkways are especially popular. Naturalistic landscapes look best with curved, flowing paths. An old rule of thumb dictates that walkways be at least four feet wide, the minimum width for two people to walk comfortably side-by-side.

Garden steps, too, require careful planning. As a general rule, the treads should be wide and the risers short. Many designers agree that each step should have a rise

of between four and five inches, and each tread should be between fourteen and sixteen inches wide. These dimensions allow a natural rhythm for ascending and descending and create proportions suitable to garden settings.

If you use a wheelbarrow in your garden, consider installing a gentle ramp (preferably with no more than a three percent grade) rather than stairs. Fully loaded wheelbarrows are notoriously unstable, and practically impossible to maneuver up or down steps.

If you plan to use your garden extensively at night, be sure to install lights along walkways and steps—hazardous areas when navigation is attempted by starlight. Keep the lights as close to the path or steps as possible, to avoid disturbing the natural quality of the nighttime landscape. For more information, see the section on Outdoor Lighting later in this chapter.

TRELLISES & SCREENS

A trellis is a latticework construction, usually made of wood, either free-standing or placed against a wall or fence. A screen, on the other hand, can be constructed of almost any material, from plastic to metal, or even composed of a group of shrubs or other plants. A screen may be placed to create a privacy "wall," to offer protection from sun and wind, or to block an undesirable view. Although trellises are used specifically as a support for vining plants, they also make excellent screens.

A trellis can be as simple or as elaborate as you care to make it. During the Renaissance, in the grand gardens of the French royalty, skilled craftsmen raised *treillage* to an art form. They created intricately patterned trellises, some designed to fool the eye with tricks of perspective. Although expensive and difficult to construct, fine treillage can still be created today. It makes a powerful design statement in a formal, elegant landscape, and is especially appropriate to houses in the French Provincial or Norman style.

A single trellis can shield a window from view, or act as both a screen and a windbreak next to a patio or deck. To screen a larger area from view, such as a vegetable garden or refuse area, a series of trellises can be placed side by side—a simple, inexpensive, and effective solution. Annual vines (scarlet runner bean, any of the morning glories, cup-and-saucer vine, or nasturtium) can be planted from seed in the spring to give quick cover for the entire warm season. Or if you prefer not to use vines, you can use lath or other lumber to create a dense design.

Given a couple of hours and the right materials, even a novice builder can construct a trellis. Stakes and lath can be purchased at most home improvement and lumber stores. If you plan to use the trellis as a support for plants, keep the design simple; most of it will be covered up in time. And remember that even delicate-looking vines can be very destructive as they grow, so make the trellis as sturdy as possible.

For an even simpler screen, consider ready-made lattice, widely available at lumber stores and garden centers. Although it's not really sturdy enough to support a growing vine, lattice makes an excellent screen just as it is. Generally available in four-by-eight-foot panels, ready-made lattice can be attached to a couple of posts or nailed to a frame and propped up from the rear. It can be stained, painted, or left to weather naturally. If you decide to paint your trellis or lattice, remember that light colors will make it stand out in the landscape, obscuring what's behind it; dark colors will make it blend into the landscape.

Besides lattice, many other types of construction material—from fiberglass panels to reed fencing available in rolls—can be used to provide screening. The choice of materials should be based on whatever is appropriate for your house and geographic area. Reed fencing may look great next to a deck in Florida, but it won't be appropriate in the rugged climate of the Rockies. Whatever you use, make sure the frame and posts are sturdy enough to withstand an occasional storm or high winds.

Living plants make the most attractive screens of all. The best screening plants are shrubby ones that branch from the base, with dense foliage. Of course, plants are also the slowest method for achieving a screen; even fast-growing ten-gallon-size plants take a couple of years to start providing privacy.

The most attractive plant screens are composed of random groupings. Except for a hedge, a straight row of shrubs looks unnatural in most landscapes. It's better to make a grouping of two or three different types of shrubs that combine nicely together, perhaps providing seasonal flowers, berries, or fall color, in addition to serving as a screen. If you need a year-round screen, be sure to select plants that do not lose their leaves during the winter.

SEATS & BENCHES

*I*f you want to make your outdoor spaces really hospitable, don't forget to include seats and benches. After all, you wouldn't expect people to spend much time in your living room if there were no place to sit down!

Garden seats and benches can be specially built to fit a certain site, or purchased ready-made from garden centers, nurseries, or catalogs. In recent years all types of garden furniture have become available—everything from recreations of period European and early American designs, to the latest contemporary furniture constructed of space-age plastics. With this great variety, it should be possible to coordinate your outdoor furniture with the style of your house. English-inspired designs look wonderful with Tudor-style houses and in gardens with a country theme. Various types of wrought-iron furniture (or, recently, "wrought" aluminum) are appropriate with French-style houses—while clean-lined plastic furniture complements contemporary homes.

Seats and benches should be placed where they will receive the most use. The most obvious spots are close to the house—on decks, patios, terraces, or balconies,

in eating, cooking, and relaxing areas. In large gardens, other locations may call for seating as well, to take advantage of a compelling view, or next to a fountain or pond. An often overlooked site is at the extreme rear of the grounds, looking back toward the house. Most people think only of sitting close to the house and looking out into the garden, but the opposite view can be very attractive. Also, a seat at the far reaches of the garden encourages people to enjoy the entire property.

Decks, patios, and terraces naturally lend themselves to built-in benches. In the case of decks and terraces, a bench placed along the perimeter can serve double duty as a railing—or triple duty, when a bench is converted to a low storage area by enclosing the sides and adding a hinged top. (However, if the deck is more than a short distance off the ground, the bench/rail will need an additional rail or backpiece for safety.) Garden retaining walls also lend themselves well to built-in benches, either on top or built into the wall itself. Benches can be incorporated into the design of raised planters, making them easier to weed and water. Even low fences and walls can become seating areas if the top is wide enough for comfort.

If you are handy with a hammer and saw, many books offer detailed plans for building a variety of outdoor furniture. One advantage to building the furniture yourself is that you can customize size and shape to fit a specific location. Be sure to select a wood that resists rotting, such as redwood, cedar, or treated fir. If you intend to paint your furniture, remember that it will probably require yearly repaintings to keep it looking good.

Whether you make your garden furniture or buy it, be sure to observe the following guidelines. If you plan to move the furniture indoors for the winter, be sure it's not too heavy or cumbersome to move easily. If you want to leave the furniture out year round, make certain it can withstand the elements. Woods known for their ability to withstand all types of weather include redwood, teak, and mahogany. Look for upholstery material fabricated of woven plastic designed to resist rotting and fading.

PLANTERS

*J*ust as outdoor living areas extend the house into the landscape, so planters—on the deck, patio, terrace, or porch—bring the landscape closer in to the house. Planters, whether free-standing or incorporated into the structure, can make your outdoor rooms more attractive and colorful. The planters themselves provide interesting accents, and even small islands of color go a long way in relieving the visual monotony of a large expanse of wooden decking or concrete.

In planning a patio or deck, consider leaving a few openings to serve as planting areas. If it's too late to incorporate open planting beds or built-in planters, check out the huge assortment of free-standing planters available at garden centers and nurseries, or custom build your own to fit a particular location.

Another variation on the planter theme is the open-bottomed box—basically a combination of free-standing planter and planting bed in which the roots of the plant can grow directly into the soil beneath the box. The advantage of this type of planter is that as trees and shrubs mature they don't outgrow their containers. Free-standing planters can take the place of railings on many decks and terraces. However, if they are too low or narrow they will not work safely as railings, particularly if children use the area.

Planters can also function as a screen or windbreak. A row of large containers with tall shrubby plants makes a perfect screen for an elevated deck that is in full view of neighboring houses. Or a row of small formal trees or shrubs trained and pruned with a single trunk (called *standards*) may be placed at the edge of a deck, terrace, or patio to visually separate one space from another without completely screening the view. Cheerful planters of annual flowers impart an atmosphere of friendliness and welcome. A long planter at the edge of a balcony with trailing, flowering plants makes a dramatic

and colorful display. Long planters are also effective placed end-to-end around a porch railing. Planters can be used to accent and clearly mark the location of a stairway, walk, or driveway.

A wide variety of both ornamental and edible plants grows well in containers, especially in courtyards where they are protected from harsh

weather. Planters filled with herbs and vegetables are nice to have close at hand in a courtyard garden, or on the back porch, deck, or patio.

Now that annuals in bloom are so widely available at nurseries, garden centers, and even grocery stores, it's easy to produce instant color for an outdoor party or special event, especially if the planters are already in place. A few dozen blooming plants can transform an ordinary deck or patio in minutes.

Large planters can be filled with a variety of flowering annuals, giving the effect of an oversized bouquet. In a free-standing planter, the best effect is achieved with the tallest flowers in the center, the medium-sized ones next, and the shortest on the outside edge, interspersed with trailing plants to drape over the side. If the planter is against a wall, the tallest flowers should go in back, the shortest in front. With a combination of plants, there's nearly always something in bloom.

On the practical side, plants require a fair amount of regular attention, and planters must be situated carefully. For example, they should drain away from the patio or deck. Some planters are lined to prevent water damage to the wood decking, and some will accommodate a drip-irrigation system.

FOUNTAINS & PONDS

*T*he sight and sound of water are natural complements to a garden setting. Flowing or still, water has the capacity to soothe the ruffled spirit. The addition of a fountain or pond can transform your garden, courtyard, or atrium into a serene and restful haven. Even the smallest area can make use of some type of water feature, if only a small recirculating wall fountain.

Among the first decisions to make is where to place the pond or fountain and whether it will have a formal or informal design. Because a waterscape is almost certain to be the focal point in any garden, thoughtful placement is very important. Formal ponds, which

rely on straight lines and geometric shapes, are often placed in full view, with no attempt to disguise the fact that they are artificial bodies of water. They can be situated in the direct line of sight from a terrace, deck, or patio with happy results. Imagine sitting in your favorite spot on the deck and letting your eye wander to such a destination. Few things are as restful to contemplate as water. Informal, natural-looking ponds are often hidden amid plantings and rocks, graced by a waterfall rather than a fountain, and designed to harmonize with the natural landscape. Another option is a reflecting pool— a still, shallow pond with no fountain or waterfall. Whether the pool is formal or informal, care should be taken with its placement so that it reflects a pleasing image.

Entering a courtyard or atrium where water is a central feature is like entering a special world. Because of the architectural nature of these spaces, a pond or fountain with a formal design usually works best—a circular, square, or rectangular shape, placed either in the center of the space or against the wall.

Ponds and fountains are natural gathering places, so be sure to include some seating for those who want to linger. In the case of a formal concrete pool, the edges can be raised high enough to function as a seating area.

Aside from being soothing, the sound of falling water can also help mask nearby traffic noise. Ears tend to hear what is closest to them, and the sound of a fountain is certainly preferable to the constant hum of cars and buses. In this way a fountain functions as a sort of privacy screen.

If you want to raise goldfish or aquatic plants, consider the following facts. Although goldfish can be extremely hardy, they obviously cannot survive in a pond that freezes solid. If you live in a cold winter climate, either bring the fish indoors for the winter or outfit the pond with a small heater like the ones used to keep birdbaths from freezing. If your new pond is constructed from concrete, wait to add fish until plants and algae are well established. If you want to grow waterlilies, the water should be still rather than recir-

culating. Most kinds of waterlilies also require full sun to produce their lavish blossoms.

You can construct a pond or reflecting pool of concrete, or purchase one made from metal, fiberglass, or a variety of plastics. If you are interested in a ready-formed pond liner, and can't find one locally, try mail-order catalogs that specialize in waterlilies and other aquatic plants. Recirculating pumps and fountain jets can be purchased at most large nurseries and garden centers. Another possibility is to simply dig a basin in the earth and line it with vinyl. Rocks along the perimeter will hold the vinyl in place and attractively outline the pond. You can also make a pond of stones bonded with cement, or use "plastic cement," a liquid that dries to look like stone.

HEARTHS

*A*lthough they are not as popular as they were a generation ago, outdoor hearths, or firepits, make good sense for those who want to spend as much time as possible outside. A hearth is a natural gathering place, especially on a chilly evening. With the addition of an adjustable grill, the fireplace can also be used for cooking. So when a hint of winter in the air hurries most folks indoors, you can continue to enjoy your outdoor space with a blazing fire.

The method used to contain the fire can be as simple as a ring of stones or as elaborate as an indoor-type fireplace, complete with hearth and chimney. If you opt for a full-fledged fireplace, consider incorporating it into a garden wall to help retain the heat from the fire and to block the wind. The wall might have built-in ledges to hold dishes and utensils. It will also provide privacy and further enhance the feeling of a true outdoor room.

Because it is a natural gathering place, the fireplace should be located where it will receive the most use,

such as on a patio or terrace close to the house. Some type of overhead protection, vented to let smoke and heat escape, will allow you to cook outdoors as much of the year as possible.

All sorts of culinary features can be part of the fireplace, including grills, griddles, ovens, and smokers. Serious outdoor chefs also require such niceties as plenty of level "counter" space, a cutting board, and an outdoor sink for easy cleanup. The more sophisticated your outdoor cooking needs, the more elaborate the plans will need to be. If you want to get into it in a big way, consult any of the recent books on building outdoor fireplaces and barbecues. Many of these books include photographs and plans, helpful whether you plan to build it yourself or simply want to show the contractor what you have in mind. These books also include technical advice, such as how to avoid the problem of wayward smoke.

If you don't want to build a permanent outdoor fireplace, consider a portable barbecue. These are ideal for use on patios and terraces, but special care should be taken to prevent accidental fires if they are used on wooden decks or under roof overhangs. With any outdoor fire, it's a good idea to keep a garden hose close at hand and a fire extinguisher attached to a nearby exterior wall.

An outdoor hearth makes a wonderful focal point for casual entertaining. A summer party might begin with a charcoal-cooked meal and end with the guests lingering around the fire long into the night. Everyone is drawn to the magic of a fire, so make sure you have plenty of comfortable chairs around the fireplace, and a good supply of firewood close at hand.

BRIDGES

*I*n purely practical terms, bridges are extensions of walkways, located where the terrain makes it impossible to build a walk, such as over a waterway or canyon. Aside from their practicality, however, bridges have a unique aesthetic appeal. Few people can resist the temptation to find out where a bridge leads, or to linger and gaze reflectively down into the water below.

Like other outdoor features, bridges may be built in various styles for different effects. An arched bridge, for instance, brings a distinctly oriental quality to a garden. It need not cross over water; it will be just as attractive spanning an artificial dry creek bed, made of large, smooth stones laid in a pattern resembling a waterway.

A couple of well-pruned trees and a stone lantern might complete the scene, offering visitors a fairly authentic recreation of an Asian garden.

A trellis of wood or metal can be added to a bridge as a support for vining plants. Although a vined trellis requires considerable upkeep in terms of pruning and training, the results are well worth it. Vines might also be trained to grow along the bottom of the bridge, softening the lines and reflecting beautifully in the water below.

Bridges serve as transitions in all parts of the landscape. A wooden bridge might connect two separate decks, perhaps on slightly different levels. The effect can be very lovely when a bridge leads through a wooded area from a larger, more public deck, to a smaller, more private one. A bridge at the front of a house, leading to the entrance, evokes images of castles, moats, and drawbridges, underscoring the transition from the world outside to the private space within.

GAZEBOS

*P*erhaps the most fanciful and romantic of outdoor structures is the gazebo, whose origins can be traced to the medieval watchtower perched on the fortress wall. To this day, the gazebo retains its ancestral function: to enable the viewer to see all around. A free-standing structure, the gazebo traditionally has a solid, peaked roof and open sides, providing an airy but shaded shelter with an unimpeded view. Ideally, the gazebo should be situated to take advantage of this characteristic, on a rise or in an especially delightful part of the garden. Because it is usually an ornate, decorative structure, the gazebo naturally becomes a focal point in the landscape, and needs to be placed with that fact in mind.

Although gazebos are commonly associated with Victorian gardens, they can be fashioned in any number of styles and designs to accompany almost any type of house and landscape.

Many people ask, "What do you do in a gazebo?" You can do anything you like, but much depends on how you furnish it. With a table and chairs, a gazebo becomes a special place for a romantic meal. It can't be beat as a place to string up a hammock, and with the addition of comfortable seating it's perfect for reading or just contemplating the glories of the garden. And children can easily transform a gazebo into anything from a performing stage to a rocket ship.

If a swimming pool is in your plans, consider a gazebo close by. You can get out of the sun for a few minutes and still keep a lookout on kids in the pool. And it's an ideal spot for serving poolside snacks. A gazebo may also be incorporated into a large deck. Raising it a few steps above the rest of the deck accentuates its "watchtower" character. Wherever it's located, the addition of

lights will make the gazebo a beautiful sight at night.

Keep plantings simple around your gazebo. Because such garden structures are so ornamental, it's self-defeating to cover them up with shrubs or vining plants. Moreover, most vines are destructive to carpentry. A simple planting of a low evergreen hedge or a compact arrangement of flowering annuals will complement the gazebo nicely without detracting from its architectural beauty.

Wooden gazebos are neither inexpensive nor particularly easy to build. However, excellent plans are available from lumber companies and from a number of books devoted solely to gazebo design and construction. If you feel that building your own is beyond your capabilities, kits are available, as well as ready-made models in a variety of materials.

OUTDOOR LIGHTING

When you have gone to the effort of creating attractive areas for outdoor living, you will want to spend as much time as you can enjoying them. One of the best ways to extend those pleasures is with the addition of outdoor lighting. New technology has made outdoor lighting easy to install and reasonable in cost, both to buy and to operate. Low-voltage systems are completely safe for outdoor use and can be installed even by those without any previous electrical experience.

When you install an outdoor lighting system, your first consideration must be safety. Outdoor spaces can be treacherous at night, and every effort should be made to provide clearly lit walkways and stairs, and to illuminate any changes in level on decks, patios, and terraces.

After you have decided *what* needs to be lighted, you can consider *how*. Outdoor lighting has its own set of aesthetic considerations. Here, one general rule applies: don't overdo it. A little bit of light goes a surprisingly long way outdoors. The point is not to light outdoor spaces as completely and brightly as you would indoor spaces, but to create instead a subtle, natural-looking nighttime scene.

Start planning your lighting scheme by imagining the landscape totally black, without any light whatsoever. Keep in mind that the goal is not to wash the entire area in even light, but rather to highlight those areas that are either a safety concern—steps, for example, or the edge of the pool—or focal points in the landscape, such as a statue, a gazebo, or a tree with a particularly attractive shape. By lighting selectively, you can accentuate the positive and leave less desirable views and objects in the dark.

For walkways, stairs, or any change in level, choose a fixture that will direct the light as close to the walk or step as possible. Avoid overhead lighting, such as a lamppost, or lighting at eye level. Any light will attract the eye, and the object here is to direct the attention to the ground below, where the hazard lies. This approach not only makes for a safer nighttime landscape, but a more beautiful one as well.

The typical installation of spotlights under the eaves to illuminate a deck or patio often casts harsh light over a wide area. It's better to light the perimeter of the deck or patio with low-voltage lights close to the ground and provide extra light for dining or cooking right where you need it, with kerosene or hurricane lamps.

In general, most outdoor lighting should be directed downward with the actual source of light as obscured as possible. Eye-level lights can be distracting because the eyes constantly try to balance extremely dark areas against extremely bright ones. One exception to this rule is when you choose to highlight a vertical element in the garden, such as a tree or a statue. In this case, lighting placed at ground level and directed upward can be very effective. If you disguise the source of the light with plants, rocks, or some other sort of screen, the scene will be even more alluring and natural-looking.

Lighting the exterior of houses is a fairly new trend and should be done with a soft touch, or the result may look more like a commercial property than a private home. This is another instance where upward-facing lights are recommended, usually placed close to the wall, pointing up to the eaves. The intent is to wash the walls with low-intensity light. If the house is not too brightly or too extensively lit the effect can be dramatic, giving the impression that the house is gently floating in an otherwise dark landscape. Before permanently installing this type of system, try experimenting over a period of several nights to determine the effects of lights placed at different locations and angles.

Frontal Sheet

Foundation Plans

Detailed Floor Plans

House Cross-Sections

Interior Elevations

Exterior Elevations

Material List

COMPLETE HOME PLANS TO HELP <u>YOU</u> PUT IT ALL TOGETHER

T he Home Planners Blueprint Package will help you and your family intelligently plan your new home. The time you spend with the detailed plans of your home will be informative and enjoyable. Most important, the plans will help you make the most of the time you spend working with your builder and architect. The Blueprint Package will save you time and money.

With each Blueprint Package you will receive detailed architect's blueprints, a material list, and a specification outline.

BLUEPRINTS

FRONTAL SHEET   Artist's landscaped sketch of the exterior and ink-line floor plans.

FOUNDATION PLAN   Basement and foundation plan in ¼-inch scale, plus plot plan for locating house on building site.

DETAILED FLOOR PLAN   First- and second-floor plans in ¼-inch scale, plus cross-section detail keys and layouts of electrical outlets and switches.

HOUSE CROSS-SECTIONS   Large-scale sections of foundation, interior and exterior walls, floors and roof details.

INTERIOR ELEVATIONS   Large-scale interior details of kitchen cabinet design, bathrooms, laundry, fireplaces, and built-ins.

EXTERIOR ELEVATIONS   Drawings in ¼-inch scale of front, rear, and sides of house.

MATERIAL LIST

Outlines the quantity, type, and size of the non-mechanical materials required to build your home. Simplifies your material ordering and gets you quicker and more accurate prices from your builder and hardware dealer. *(Material List not available separately.)*

Includes:
- Masonry, Veneer & Fireplace
- Framing Lumber
- Roofing & Sheet Metal
- Windows & Door Frames
- Exterior Trim & Insulation
- Tile & Flooring
- Interior Trim, Kitchen Cabinets
- Rough & Finish Hardware

Because of differences in geographical regions, local codes, and installation methods, mechanical materials and specifications are not included. Consult local heating, plumbing, and electrical contractors for the necessary materials take-offs for your home.

SPECIFICATION OUTLINE

A 16-page fill-in specification list of more than 150 phases of home construction from excavating to painting. Lets you tell your builder the exact materials, equipment, and methods of construction you want in your new home. *Additional outlines are $3.00 a copy.*

Includes:
- General Instructions, Suggestions, & Information
- Excavating & Grading
- Masonry
- Concrete Work
- Sheet Metal Work
- Carpentry, Millwork, & Roofing
- Lath & Plaster or Drywall Wallboard
- Schedule for Room Finishes
- Painting & Finishing
- Tile
- Electrical
- Plumbing
- Heating & Air-Conditioning

BEFORE YOU ORDER

1. STUDY THE DESIGNS
As you review the custom homes in this and other Home Planners books, keep in mind the total living requirements of your family, both indoors and out. Although we do not modify plans for our customers, minor changes can be made before you start construction. If you plan to make major changes, you should order one set of blueprints and have them redrawn locally. Consult with your builder or architect if you plan major changes.

2. HOW TO ORDER BLUE-PRINTS
Complete the order form below and return it with your remittance. Credit card and C.O.D. orders are accepted. For C.O.D. shipments, the post office will collect all charges, including postage and C.O.D. fees. C.O.D. shipments are not permitted outside the United States. Telephone orders can be processed and shipped in the next day's mail. Call toll free 1-800-521-6797. Michigan residents call collect 0-313-477-1854.

3. REVERSE BLUEPRINTS
As a special service to those wishing to build in reverse of the plan as shown, Home Planners offers reverse blueprints at a cost of $25.00 additional per set with each order. Although the lettering and dimensions appear backwards, reverse blueprints are a valuable reference because they show the house as it's actually being built.

4. EXCHANGE POLICY
Since blueprints are printed in response to individual orders, blueprint materials are not returnable. However, the first set of blueprints in any order, or the one set in a single-set order, may be exchanged for a set of another design for $20.00 plus $3.00 postage and handling via surface mail; $4.00 for priority mail.

HOW MANY SETS OF BLUEPRINTS WILL YOU NEED?

A single set of blueprints of your favorite design is sufficient if you plan to study the house in greater detail. However, if you are planning to get estimates or to build, you may need as many as seven sets of blueprints. You can save by planning your order carefully and ordering your total requirements now. The first set of blueprints is $125.00, and additional sets of the same design in each order are $30.00. To determine the number of sets you will need, use the check list below.

_____ **OWNER'S SET**

_____ **BUILDER** (usually requires 3 sets: legal, inspection, tradesperson)

_____ **BUILDING PERMIT** (occasionally requires 2 sets)

_____ **MORTGAGE SOURCE** (usually 1 set for conventional; 3 sets for F.H.A. and V.A.)

_____ **REVIEW BOARD OR SUBDIVISION COMMITTEE**

_____ **TOTAL NUMBER OF SETS REQUIRED**

HOME PLANNERS, INC., 23761 Research Dr., Farmington Hills, MI 48024

Please rush me the following:

_____ SET(S) BLUEPRINTS FOR DESIGN NO(S). _____ $ _____
Single Set, $125.00; Additional Identical Sets in Same Order $30.00 ea.
4 Set Package of Same Design, $175.00 (Save $40.00)
8 Set Package of Same Design, $225.00 (Save $110.00)
(Material Lists and 1 Specification Outline included)
_____ SPECIFICATION OUTLINES @ $3.00 EACH $ _____

Michigan Residents add 4% sales tax $ _____

| FOR POSTAGE AND HANDLING PLEASE CHECK ✔ & REMIT | ☐ $3.00 Added to Order for Surface Mail (UPS) – Any Order
☐ $4.00 Added for Priority Mail of One-Three Sets of Blueprints.
☐ $6.00 Added for Priority Mail of Four or more Sets of Blueprints.
☐ For Canadian orders add $2.00 to above applicable rates. | } $ _____ |

☐ C.O.D. PAY POSTMAN (C.O.D. Within U.S.A. Only) TOTAL in U.S.A. funds $ _____

PLEASE PRINT
Name _____
Street _____
City _____ State _____ Zip _____

CREDIT CARD ORDERS ONLY: Fill in the boxes below. **Prices subject to change without notice.**

Credit Card No. ☐☐☐☐☐☐☐☐☐☐☐☐☐☐ Expiration Date Month/Year ☐☐☐☐

CHECK ONE: ☐ **VISA** ☐ **MasterCard**

Order Form Key TBIOBP Your Signature _____

BLUEPRINT ORDERS SHIPPED WITHIN 48 HOURS OF RECEIPT!

HOME PLANNERS, INC., 23761 Research Dr., Farmington Hills, MI 48024

Please rush me the following:

_____ SET(S) BLUEPRINTS FOR DESIGN NO(S). _____ $ _____
Single Set, $125.00; Additional Identical Sets in Same Order $30.00 ea.
4 Set Package of Same Design, $175.00 (Save $40.00)
8 Set Package of Same Design, $225.00 (Save $110.00)
(Material Lists and 1 Specification Outline included)
_____ SPECIFICATION OUTLINES @ $3.00 EACH $ _____

Michigan Residents add 4% sales tax $ _____

| FOR POSTAGE AND HANDLING PLEASE CHECK ✔ & REMIT | ☐ $3.00 Added to Order for Surface Mail (UPS) – Any Order
☐ $4.00 Added for Priority Mail of One-Three Sets of Blueprints.
☐ $6.00 Added for Priority Mail of Four or more Sets of Blueprints.
☐ For Canadian orders add $2.00 to above applicable rates. | } $ _____ |

☐ C.O.D. PAY POSTMAN (C.O.D. Within U.S.A. Only) TOTAL in U.S.A. funds $ _____

PLEASE PRINT
Name _____
Street _____
City _____ State _____ Zip _____

CREDIT CARD ORDERS ONLY: Fill in the boxes below. **Prices subject to change without notice.**

Credit Card No. ☐☐☐☐☐☐☐☐☐☐☐☐☐☐ Expiration Date Month/Year ☐☐☐☐

CHECK ONE: ☐ **VISA** ☐ **MasterCard**

Order Form Key TBIOBP Your Signature _____

BLUEPRINT ORDERING HOTLINE

PHONE TOLL FREE:
1-800-521-6797

Orders received by 11 a.m. (Eastern standard time) will be processed the same day and shipped the following day. Michigan residents call collect 0-313-477-1854.

NOTE: When ordering by phone, please mention the Order Form Key Number located in the box at the lower left corner of the blueprint order form.

In Canada mail orders to:
HOME PLANNERS, INC.
20 Cedar Street North
Kitchener, Ontario N2H 2W8
Phone: 519-743-4169

ADDITIONAL PLAN BOOKS

THE DESIGN CATEGORY SERIES

360 TWO STORY HOMES English Tudors, Early American Salt Boxes, Gambrels, Farmhouses, Southern Colonials, Georgians, French Mansards, Contemporaries. Floor plans for small and large families. Two to 6 bedrooms, family rooms, libraries, extra baths, mudrooms. Homes for all budgets. **288 Pages, $6.95**

(1)

150 1½ STORY HOMES Cape Cod, Williamsburg, Georgian, Tudor, Contemporaries. Low-budget and country-estate feature sections. Expandable family plans. Formal and informal living and dining areas. Spacious country kitchens. Indoor-outdoor livability with covered porches and functional terraces. **128 Pages, $3.95**

(2)

210 ONE STORY HOMES OVER 2,000 SQ. FT. Spanish, Western, Tudor, French, Contemporaries. Family rooms, separate dining rooms, atriums, efficient kitchens, laundries. Designs from modest to country-estate budgets. **192 Pages, $4.95**

(3)

315 ONE STORY HOMES UNDER 2,000 SQ. FT. An outstanding selection of traditional and contemporary exteriors for medium and restricted budgets. Efficient, practical floor plans. Gathering rooms, formal and informal living and dining rooms, mudrooms, indoor-outdoor livability. Economy homes. **192 Pages, $4.95**

(4)

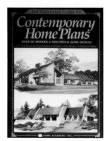

215 MULTI-LEVEL HOMES A large variety of exterior styles and floor plans for flat and sloping sites. Exposed lower levels. Balconies and decks. Upper-level lounges. Sloping ceilings. Functional outdoor terraces. **192 Pages, $4.95**

(5)

223 VACATION HOMES A-Frames, Chalets, Hexagons, and designs with decks, balconies, and terraces. Oriented for flat and sloping sites. Spacious, open planning for lakeshore or woodland living. Sleeping for 2 to 22. Lodges for summer and winter use. **176 Pages, $4.95**

(6)

OTHER CURRENT TITLES

330 EARLY AMERICAN HOME PLANS Complete collection of Early American and Traditional homes in one magnificent book! Traces early American architecture from colonial times to traditional styles popular today. An outstanding array of Gambrels, Salt Boxes, Cape Cods, Georgian and Federal variations, Southern Colonials, Farmhouses and Country Estate houses. **304 Pages, $9.95**

(7)

335 CONTEMPORARY HOME PLANS The definitive statement on modern and functional home designs! Offers a colorful guide to modern architecture, including a history of contemporary American styling. Features Solar-Oriented Trend Houses, Earth-Sheltered Homes and Atrium Designs, as well as imaginative plans for one-, 1½-, two-story and multi-level Contemporaries. **304 Pages, $9.95**

(8)

ENCYCLOPEDIA OF HOME DESIGNS – 450 PLANS The best-selling home plan encyclopedia of all time! Varying exterior styles plus practical floor plans for all building budgets. Formal-informal living patterns. Indoor-outdoor livability. Small, growing, and large family home plans. One of the largest selections of home plans available in a single volume. Over 1,150 illustrations and lavish use of color. **320 Pages, $9.95**

(9)

HOME PLANNERS, INC., 23761 Research Drive, Farmington Hills, Michigan 48024

Please mail me the following:

THE DESIGN CATEGORY SERIES

1. _____ 360 Two Story Homes @ $6.95 ea. $ _____
2. _____ 150 1½ Story Homes @ $3.95 ea. $ _____
3. _____ 210 One Story Homes Over 2,000 Sq. Ft. @ $4.95 $ _____
4. _____ 315 One Story Homes Under 2,000 Sq. Ft. @ $4.95 $ _____
5. _____ 215 Multi-Level Homes @ $4.95 ea. $ _____
6. _____ 223 Vacation Homes @ $4.95 ea. $ _____

ALL 6 BOOKS, OVER 1,250 DESIGNS, 1,168 PAGES ONLY $19.95 (A $30.70 VALUE. SAVE $10.75) $ _____

OTHER CURRENT TITLES

7. _____ 330 Early American Home Plans @ $9.95 $ _____
8. _____ 335 Contemporary Home Plans @ $9.95 $ _____
9. _____ 450 House Plans Encyclopedia @ $9.95 ea. $ _____

Subtotal $ _____
Michigan residents add 4% Sales Tax $ _____
Postage and Handling $ __$1.00__
TOTAL – Check Enclosed $ _____

MAIL TODAY – Satisfaction Guaranteed! Your Order Will Be Processed and Shipped Within 48 Hours!

PLEASE PRINT

Name _____

Address _____

City _____ State _____ Zip _____

In Canada Mail To: Home Planners, Inc., 20 Cedar St. North, Kitchener, Ontario N2H 2W8

TBIOBK

INDEXES